Reviving
Fatherhood

Reviving Fatherhood

Guiding Every Dad from First Steps to Lasting Legacy

STEVEN KOLBERG

Get Your Free Gift!

Thank you for joining me on this journey of fatherhood! Your commitment to becoming a better dad is inspiring, and as a token of my appreciation, I'd like to offer you a special gift. Visit revivedbrand.com/promo to claim your exclusive gift!

This resource is designed to complement the principles we discuss in this book, providing you with practical tips, insights, and actionable steps. It will further support you in reclaiming your identity in Jesus and redefining your role as a father, helping you lead your family with intention and purpose.

I'm excited for you to dive deeper and continue this transformative journey!

You can get a copy by visiting:
www.revivedbrand.com/promo

I am dedicating this book to my wife, Kelly, and all my wonderful children. My hope and prayer is that God uses the words in this book to help shape your lives to become more like him. Never stop learning and always be humble.

Contents

Introduction

It was about 2:00 a.m. I was in a place that was unfamiliar to me. On about an hour of sleep in the last forty-eight hours, I needed to be on my A game at a second's notice. The stakes were too high, and the cost was too great for me to not be prepared for what was about to take place. It was eerily silent, as dark as the night could get, and as unknown a situation as any could prepare for. I heard the sound I was preparing for: cries from my newborn son. He awoke from his slumber needing someone to come to his aid.

At this moment in time, there were two decisions on the table facing me: (1) as exhausted as I was, I could let my wife deal with it, or (2) I could sacrifice my personal desires, such as wanting to sleep, and get up and help. Wrestling with what decision to make, I couldn't make up my mind. I always told myself before I had kids that I wanted to set a foundation of fatherhood that was different from the messages society and culture preached to me about what it means to be a father. But being exhausted and selfishly wanting sleep challenged that dream I had for myself. Finally, the wrestling match was settled. I decided I was going to be the father I wanted to be, believed I should be, and not cower away to society's expectations of fatherhood.

So I slowly stood up; stumbled around, trying to find my glasses; and carefully and quietly, avoiding disturbing my sleeping wife, shuffled my way toward my son's bassinet in the post-delivery hospital room. Opening different drawers and feeling around, I was in search of diapers and wipes. Finally! I found what I was looking for, and I got to work. After I unswaddled James, I took off the diaper, replaced the diaper, and reswaddled him. James was satisfied, so I placed him back down, and he drifted back off to sleep.

"I can't believe I did that!" I thought. I remembered promising myself I would never change a diaper until it was my own kid. I felt a sense of pride wash over me, having fulfilled that promise to myself. It was like I just finished my initiation into fatherhood. Having just changed my first diaper, I was reminded from seeing my peacefully sleeping child that I was exhausted, and I needed to get what sleep I could before I was needed again to come to the rescue.

Several hours later in the early morning, the nurse came in for the routine check-in, and while in the room, she decided to change James's diaper. I was so happy to get a break and rest some more. I closed my eyes and drifted back off to sleep.

In the morning around 6:30 a.m., a nurse came back in when my wife and I were awake to let us in on the night's events and how James was doing. "All things are good, except one issue," the nurse noted. I sat up. "The diaper was on backward. Not even sure how you managed to do that," she said in the most backhanded, insulting kind of way.

"Wow, okay," I thought. "You didn't have to be so rude about it."

Okay, probably a bit of exaggeration and she probably wasn't that rude, but after a forty-plus-hour labor, little to no sleep, and my first diaper change ever, my ability to read the situation was depleted, gone, nada. I still took it as an insult like she knew I changed the diaper. I tried to imagine what she was thinking. Thoughts filled my mind:

"Why did you even try?"

"Leave the baby stuff to the moms . . . "

"Guys are dumb when it comes to being a dad."

"Dads are not really supposed to be involved anyway."

"James would have been better off with Mom changing the diaper; she actually knows what to do."

Looking back at it, I wondered why I assumed these thoughts. I didn't have to think long. That is what culture and society scream at dads daily. Whenever men see other dads changing diapers, playing with their kids, or holding babies, it seems unnatural or not the manly way. The voices from the crowd yell that manliness and fatherhood means "leaving the kids to the mom." Your job is to just work, put food on the table, and discipline the kids when they disrespect Mom. These messages are anything but encouraging to men and especially first-time dads.

Culture says this, Christian culture says that, and I think God is leading me this way. It was a mess to try to sort out and took lots of work and help from God. This is what eventually led to me writing this book. How can I help prepare other men to be in a better place than where I was when fatherhood became my world?

I won't mince words: I disagree with culture. This could not be further from the truth when it comes to dads and the roles they should have in their kids' lives, especially in the infant years. We need to tear down the culture's definition of dad and create a new one. Dads should be changing diapers, taking kids to appointments, staying up all night with them when sick, playing on the ground after a long day of work, feeding them bottles, making formula, getting up at night, and the list goes on. Since most men are listening to culture's definition of fatherhood, this leaves wives carrying responsibilities like this on their own, and that is wrong. However, these are not exclusive tasks for dads to do either; instead, this is a joint effort with our wives. Neither parent is meant to carry this alone.

I did not come up with these examples on my own, and it is not only my opinion that this is the way it should be. It is the truth I found from the source of truth: the Bible. No, the Bible does not say to bottle-feed the baby or set up the baby swing, but the Creator of the universe, Creator of me, and Creator of my kids wrote the truths of life in his book. This is where I found what it is to be a dad and why it includes doing these things.

My son, James, from this story is now four years old, and it seems like a decade ago I changed my first diaper. During these four years, I was also blessed with a daughter, June, who is a joyful two-year-old, and her sister, Jovi, is our newest, freshest family member. There have been many learning curves and adventures along the way.

Over the past four years, I have learned many lessons about being a dad and what changes it has on your life. Going from married to married with kids is a huge transition in life, and I was not prepared. You think you just wake up married and it's sunshine and rainbows? Heck no! Every married man can nod in agreement on this.

Watching my first child be born, I had no idea the work that would be required of me. Doing the math for other responsibilities I had accumulated, I was unprepared and learning on the fly. I was wandering through a marsh with tall cattails blocking my view and making it challenging to navigate my way.

I wrestled with identity, priorities, and mental health and felt like I had no tools in my belt to get me through fatherhood. No one equips men for what it takes or means to be a father, much less prepares us to leave a legacy that lasts.

There came a point about three years in when I noticed I had more of a bird's-eye view of the playing field of fatherhood. After being in the trenches of a new dad for so long, it was refreshing to be able to have a different perspective. Imagine a drone flying up into the sky and overlooking the playing field down below. Clarity began to form in front of my eyes and in my mind. I noticed there were players in the field, there was strategy to be decided, and there were tools to get you through the different situations one would face.

In beautiful Aspen, Colorado, God dropped a thought right into my head that would change the course of my life. It was to write about everything I have learned about being a dad. I pondered it for a while, then concluded I would write the book. Everything I have discovered that lays the foundation of fatherhood is in this book. To keep my insights to myself from what I have learned would be cruel and heartless to other fathers since I know it is already so hard to be a dad. I want every dad, and especially every new dad, who reads this book to (1) feel more confident in their abilities to be a father, and (2) know that they can do it!

Deep down, I know we all want to be the best fathers we can be and leave a lasting legacy. But the question we all face is: How? How do we revive fatherhood from what seems like an impossible place with culture's messages? Any solid building has a solid foundation. So the best way to have a lasting legacy as an impactful father many years from now is to lay the best foundations today.

Don't believe me? I do not want you to figure it out on your own like I had to. If there had been a way to read this book myself before or after my children were born, I would have avoided so many pitfalls and potholes and gained the guidance I searched for earlier in my fatherhood journey. My desire for you is to avoid as many of the same obstacles as possible.

There are enough detours and roads to navigate in fatherhood—the burden of "How do I set myself up for success?" should not be one of them. Wrestling with your identity, confidence, or your relationships, including your relationship with yourself, only adds to the weight we feel.

I promise, if you put into practice and follow the guiding insights I provide in this book, four things will happen.

1) You will know what it is to be a dad and have more peace, confidence, rest, and self-worth in yourself and your abilities as a husband and father. Your life will be forever changed in ways your mind cannot even begin to imagine.

2) Your family will gain a leader who is prepared and equipped for the road ahead. They will be impacted by your peace, comfort, rest, security, and confidence.

3) Those in your circle will be impacted. People are always watching; they will see a transformed man.

4) Your impactful legacy will extend in and through your kids and beyond your four walls. A small domino effect of change today has the power to course-correct the history of tomorrow.

Are you thinking these are too bold? Perhaps you are saying, "Oh, wow, Steven. Those are bold promises, and I doubt you can actually promise that." And . . . you are correct!

If it were my words and opinions you are about to read in this book, I would never make a bold promise like this. But this book is written from exploring the truth of the universe according to the Creator himself, God. I know without a shadow of a doubt that when God enters the equation, circumstances beyond our wildest dreams become realities, and the impossible becomes possible. A lost legacy becomes an impactful legacy. Broken relationships become healed. A dying life can become revived.

I warn you, though: The longer you wait, the less time you have to start putting into practice what you learn. To grow in something, requires time and discipline. If you are disciplined to implement what you learn but do not give it time, you will never see results. If you give it time but do not discipline yourself to put it into practice, then there will be no growth. I urge you to not put off reading this book and implementing what you learn. If you are a dad already or a dad-to-be, the perfect starting point is now.

My questions to you now are: Do you want to change? Do you want to change not only yourself, but also the world around you? Current dads, are you tired of the same old dance and routine that are not working? Dads-to-be, are you fearful you may end up falling into culture's lackluster definition of dad? All dads, do you want the seemingly impossible?

Then read this book, following its guide to the very last sentence, and apply everything you learn from what God teaches you. You will journey through three sections in this book: the key players, priority management, and tools and strategies for success.

I have two disclaimers before we start this journey together.

1) Be careful; we do not want to get self-focused. When we become all-consumed with us and our story and processing our life, it takes our eyes off Jesus. Only true and life-giving fulfillment comes from when our eyes are fixated on him alone. Don't let your eyes, being focused on yourself, rob you of your joy. Sure, we are all not going to live out what God teaches us perfectly, but that doesn't mean we need to beat ourselves up, feel depressed, and not even try. Instead, let's keep our eyes on Jesus and the hope he offers that life change is possible through our pursuit of him. I believe out of the overflow of this pursuit, the characteristics we need to develop as men and fathers will naturally fall into place.

2) God is a God of redemption. The whole story of the Bible is about his plan of redemption for humanity. It is in his nature and character. So even if you disqualify yourself because of the stage of life you are in or through mistakes made, it is never too late to let God redeem your life or your parenting.

Are you ready to start becoming the dad that God has created, called, and chosen you to be? Then turn the page to our first section, which begins with the ultimate character in our story: the greatest Father.

PART 1

THE KEY PLAYERS

CHAPTER 1

The Greatest Father

"I have no idea what I am doing," I mumbled to myself as I walked away from my son's bedroom having endured the bedtime routine. When he was three years old, my son believed he ran the world and I was to enjoy whatever he decided was right to do. Night after night, I endured complicated emotions dealing with countless questions, seemingly endless disobedience, and a comical attitude. In one night, I went from being happy, to being irritated, to having gut-roll laughter, to being angry, to being ashamed (from my anger), and it would repeat. I have often dreamed, "It would be nice if there were some map, rule book, or even a pamphlet that could guide me through this challenging adventure of parenthood, more specifically fatherhood."

After I rested from the nighttime put down, I decided to dwell on my thoughts. I came to realize, being a Christ follower, I have been given the guide that I desired: the Bible. More thoughts started spilling into my mind. "What is my purpose as a father?" "Am I supposed to act a certain way?" "Does the Bible outline the recipe for success in fatherhood?"

Ultimately I pondered the question, "Who is God, and what does he have to say about being a father?"

I decided I must start at the beginning. God is the first Father, and in order to know who I am to become, I must first learn about the greatest one. Who is God, what is his will for creation, what is his character, and what makes him a father? Understanding these questions is the vital starting point in our journey to knowing and becoming the fathers we were created to be.

We will split this chapter into two parts to learn about God. In the first part, we will assume the role of Adam in the story as a human being in God's creation. This is where we will learn about who God is and his will for us as humanity and fathers. In the second section, we will be mirroring the character of God as it practically applies to us dads.

Let's start at the very beginning of life itself, Genesis 1:1: "In the beginning God created the heavens and the earth. The earth was formless and empty, and darkness covered the deep waters. And the Spirit of God was hovering over the surface of the waters."

God was here before all of existence consisting of power and creativity. He lives in the heavens surrounded by angelic beings. He is known as the Alpha and Omega, the beginning and end. We know he is a God of creativity because the rest of Genesis 1 shares the creation story and how he created all we know and see today. The best part of all creation was his plan to form man. We were made in his image and likeness and were brought to life with his breath. God's very breath is life, and without it, we would be nothing. With his breath in the man's lungs, he then gave him direction and responsibility. Adam, the first man, did not have to wonder what his purpose was.

God is our Father, and we are his sons. Our bodies are full of his breath, and we have been given directions and responsibilities as dads and simply humans. Have you ever wondered what your purpose is as a dad or just in general? I bet most of us have. God actually provides us with a characteristic to mirror here. He doesn't leave his children without clear direction and responsibility. This clarity filled Adam with purpose for existence and led him to know what was most important to pursue in life. Lots of us would call this God's will for our life.

Knowing his purpose from his given direction and responsibilities, Adam was able to understand God's will. Look at this story a bit more. In a perfect and pure world before sin, Adam was able to feel great pleasure and happiness in a garden paradise. I mean, how could one not? Talking with God, Adam spent time growing their relationship through their walks and talks in the garden. Looking around at the splendor of the garden and life that was created, I would guarantee that Adam continually expressed his gratitude to God. God even knew Adam was lonely and created a helper for him, a beautiful woman named Eve. If you were all alone in the world and you suddenly woke up next to a gorgeous naked woman, I think the words "Thank you, Lord!" would roll right off your lips! Can you see what God willed for Adam and all his creation? He willed for his creation to be pure without sin, in a state of joy, in relationship, and on the receiving end of their praise and gratitude.

Many years later, Paul wrote something very similar in the New Testament: "Always be joyful. Never stop praying. Be thankful in all circumstances, for this is God's will for you who belong to Christ Jesus" (1 Thess. 5:16–18). Here Paul lists in simple terms what Adam was experiencing in the beginning.

In Hebrews 12, the author writes to live a holy life. Several other places in the New Testament mention pursuing a pure life. In the Old and New Testaments, we are able to see that God's will for our life means pursuing a life that is holy and pure, choosing joy, growing our relationship with God, and expressing our gratitude and thanks to him.

Before moving on, let's tie this together. We as humans are blessed by God, knowing what his will for us is. It gives us a sense of purpose to get out of bed every day. In all we do, and especially in fatherhood, we are to pursue a pure life with God, choosing joy in the midst of every circumstance while always expressing gratitude to God. This clarity of direction for life is given to us from our Father, and we must pass it down to our children.

Now that we know briefly about God and his will, we probably want to know what he is like and what characteristics there are that we can mirror for our own families. I mean, if we do not know who he is, why would we want to pursue what he wills for us? There is so much to God's character that I wouldn't be doing anyone any favors if I wrote he can be summed up in a single word or sentence. However, I do notice that he has a couple of traits that are very practical to us as fathers. Those are grace and love. All through the Bible, we see story after story revealing his character. In stories from the beginning of the Old Testament, like Noah, we see God show the character of grace by not wiping all of humanity off the face of the earth. In stories from the New Testament, we see his love displayed through the sacrifice of his son for us. Let's investigate these two characteristics a bit more.

Grace—unmerited and undeserved favor and provision: "And God will generously provide all you need. Then you will always have everything you need and plenty left over to share with others" (2 Cor. 9:8). Why would God give generously all that we need? What did we do to earn it? The answer is grace.

The character of God is to bless without reason. He chooses to lavish on us what we need just because. It feels weird to write this, as I am still trying to wrap my head around this topic myself. Another piece I want to point out here is that he does not just give what we need; he also gives more than we would ever need. Let's get practical here for a moment, and let me share a story about how I experienced God's grace in a place none other than the Home Depot.

I embarked on a journey to the Home Depot to find some cheap twenty-buck blackout shades for my son's room. As I mentioned his troublesome bedtime routine earlier, this was an attempt to help me find some peace of mind. I figured a nice dark room should help him go to sleep peacefully. In the store, I was wandering around for about thirty minutes with my nine-month-old daughter, who had just pooped herself, and James, way past his naptime. To abandon the mission would be devastating. Shedding blood, sweat, and tears to get this far, I could not quit now. I told myself I could not leave until I found the blinds because of the hardship it was to get to the store, much less wandering around aimlessly looking for them. I even pulled up the store directory on my phone to find the correct aisle and bay they were in, but no luck. Fortunately, when I was about to give up and go home defeated, an employee was able to assist me. We confirmed together that there were, in fact, no more of the cheap twenty-dollar paper blackout shades, and I was distraught. The next best option was ninety-dollar high-end shades; my budget said, "No, we definitely can't afford those!"

To provide a little necessary backstory, the budget that we were sticking to as a family was new to us this year.

"Do you want these?" The employee was waiting for my response. Unsure of myself, I nodded and uttered with despair, "Sure." It was only two seconds later that an off-duty manager happened to be walking by and witnessed the situation. Turning toward the employee, he spoke. "Hook him up. We are out of the ones he wanted, so give him those at the price of what he was looking for." My jaw hit the floor! What just happened? Making eye contact with the employee, I realized that we both were on the same page and that the manager couldn't mean what he had just said. But he repeated himself and made it very clear that I was supposed to get the high-end, ninety-dollar blackout shades for the original twenty dollars I was planning on spending. Now that was God's grace!

Leading up to this moment in time, I had not been stewarding the financial resources that God had given us the best, and this felt like the last thing I deserved. I mean, if I couldn't steward money well, why would God bless me with a financial gift like this? But now, isn't that the definition of grace? I did nothing to deserve God's favor, and he gave me way more than I was asking for. I experienced God's grace fueled by his love for me. It's an interesting phrase, grace fueled by love. Now that we know all about grace, let's tackle the topic of God's love.

God's love is the very epicenter of our existence. If it weren't for his love to share himself with creation, God would not have formed the earth and all of life. As I share this definition of love, start picturing God with these amazing attributes. The perfect definition of love can be found in 1 Corinthians 13:4–7: "Love is patient and kind. Love is not jealous or boastful or proud or rude. It does not demand its own way. It is not irritable, and it keeps no record of being wronged. It does not rejoice about injustice but rejoices whenever the truth wins out. Love never gives up, never loses faith, is always hopeful, and endures through every circumstance."

How many of us picture God this way? My guess is not many. Well, I will give us some credit. I think we picture God as maybe a handful of these words, depending on what has transpired in our lives. Dwell on these descriptions of love for a moment with me. Different from a feeling, isn't it? From reading these words Paul wrote to the church in Corinth, we conclude that love is an action and not a noun. Love is a choice, not a feeling. God, the first and greatest Father, chooses to love us perfectly, no matter what we have done, are currently doing, or will do with our lives. This includes the way we treat him as well.

This is the love of the perfect Father. Patiently and with kindness, he draws near. When he is with us, there is no jealousy, and he is not boasting of his greatness. He carries himself with honor, and we can sense his humility. Keeping a calm composure through all we do, he does not demand his way of us. Much more, he does not keep score of what we have done against him. Burdened by injustice, he presses hard for the truth and rejoices greatly for it! Most importantly, our heavenly Father never ever gives up on us, no matter the cost to him. His hope for us is unmatched; he knows us; he created us in our mothers' wombs in the secret place (Psalm 139). Even to the point of enduring the cross, in every circumstance, his choice to love us cannot be stopped. Relentlessly pursuing our souls, God embodies grace fueled by love. Love is the power to unleash grace!

What is a good or tangible image of grace and love in a person? Or how can we connect these two traits into a single character trait that we can see play out? The answer is found in the Gospel of John in the personified version of God: Jesus.

Let's look at this Scripture from John 10:14–16: "I am the good shepherd; I know my own sheep, and they know me, just as my Father knows me and I know the Father. So I sacrifice my life for the sheep. I have other sheep, too, that are not in this sheepfold. I must bring them also. They will listen to my voice, and there will be one flock with one shepherd."

Jesus references himself as a shepherd. When I picture a shepherd or, as Jews would have in that day in age, lowly nobodies out in the middle of nowhere come to mind. If you do some research, that is pretty much a definition of a shepherd. However, there is a deeper meaning behind this. If we just look on the surface, we do not see much, but let's look deeper at the heart of a shepherd, particularly in the way Jesus describes it.

In this, Jesus is explaining that we are sheep and I am tempted to feel insulted. Have you ever watched YouTube shorts or TikToks on sheep? They are dumb! So I won't get caught up in the analogy of being a dumb animal. I will look deeper. Honestly, I think dumb is a good comparison. I live my life thinking I know how to do everything the best, I can do everything on my own, and I never need anyone's help (most of the time). Don't believe me? Next time you have to go somewhere unfamiliar, ask for directions. Gotcha! We all know we guys do not ask for directions. So it is with this mentality that I go wandering off and do my own thing all the time. I bet Jesus looks at me and sighs for the millionth time when he has to go rescue me from whatever ravine I got myself stuck in, especially if it is one he just pulled me out of. But I do not think he is irritated or annoyed; as we just learned, he is grace and love. It is his choice to lavish these gifts on us.

Jesus knows his sheep; he knows me. He knows the ones who are in the pen and the ones who are not. He sacrifices for the sheep, even the ones who are gone. You hear all the time that the greatest love anyone can show is that someone lays down their life for another; that is sacrifice. Being willing to do that for others who are "not in your pen" or "obeying your commands" is a very gracious act. So instead of viewing Jesus as a smelly nobody in the middle of a field, picture him looking over you, ready to sacrifice for you at a moment's notice, no matter what you may have done or are doing.

It is with this that I present to you the template of fatherhood, God himself, a perfect Good Shepherd. It's a high bar, I know, but we must not let that scare us from looking to him as our example to follow. Sometimes I wonder if it is even worth it since I know I can't come close to being a father like God. When thoughts like this come, though, I find myself thinking about God's grace and love toward me. I am reminded that his grace is going to be my ability to love, parent, and shepherd like him. I am also comforted knowing that even in all my failures, past, present, and future, I will have this same grace and love surrounding me and following me all the days of my life.

I also remember my earthly dad when I am in these moments. My father is a man who embodies to me what it means to be a father like Jesus. Actually, just like Jesus adopts us into his family, my dad was able to adopt me from Lithuania when I was about eighteen months old and bring me into his loving family. While growing up, I saw my dad live every day, no matter what he was doing, with the purpose we talked about earlier that God provides us. He pursued and still pursues a pure life and relationship with God with his every being. I noticed him choosing joy in the midst of some very difficult circumstances, but above all, I will always remember his expressing of gratitude to God, no matter what came his way. He still does this to this day, and it is another example I hold tight to. I could write a whole chapter about my dad and all the ways his impact has forever shaped my life. In all honesty, there is a good chance I would not be writing this book if I did not have the practical and tangible guidance and example of my dad in my everyday life, showing me who Jesus was and mirroring him in the role of a father. God revived my experience of fatherhood by giving me my dad. I went from being fatherless to having a father, and it was all at the hand of God.

What about your earthly father? I know we all do not have fathers like I did growing up, but for those of us who did, that is a man deserving of your honor and respect, and is an example to follow. If you had a dad you would not want to give a second thought to, who was a strong mentor in your life that you would say was like a dad to you, or whom you viewed as one?

One of the best things we can give our children is a practical example of what it looks like to become more like Jesus. When we intentionally spend time with him, we will start to mirror who Jesus is to our children, and they will get to know who he is not by what we say but by what we do.

I do not want to pass up an important fact to acknowledge. Many of us dads often wrestle with discouragement when it comes to our parenting journey. We feel that we are failures, we can never do things right, and we just screwed up our kids; these are daily wrestling matches in our minds. Turning this discouragement into an encouragement, I want to remind us of this valuable truth. We will not parent perfectly like God, but we will have the choice to believe in God as our source of strength to continue.

How is it possible that God can be our source of strength? It is through the power of the Holy Spirit inside us. It is through his power and his alone that we will be able to become the kind of fathers we want to be. Sacrificing, teaching, training, protecting, encouraging, motivating, loving, and leading as fathers will all come to us from the greatest, perfect Father if we are willing to submit our lives to him and let him be the ruler and authority over us.

If you want this power from God, it is possible for you! By placing your faith in God and surrendering to him, you will find freedom and the strength to become who you were designed to be. You will be filled with the Holy Spirit, and the same power that raised Christ from the dead will now live in you!

Ephesians 1:19–20 states, " I also pray that you will understand the incredible greatness of God's power for us who believe him. This is the same mighty power that raised Christ from the dead and seated him in the place of honor at God's right hand in the heavenly realms."

All you have to do is believe that Jesus is who he says he is and repent. Believe that he died on the cross for your sins and in three days, rose again, defeating sin and death, bridging the gap between humanity and God once and for all. Through Jesus, it is possible to be reunited with God. See what Jesus himself says here from the book of John:

- John 3:16: "For this is how God loved the world: He gave his one and only Son, so that everyone who believes in him will not perish but have eternal life."

- John 3:18–21: "Whoever believes in him is not condemned, but whoever does not believe stands condemned already because they have not believed in the name of God's one and only Son. This is the verdict: Light has come into the world, but people loved darkness instead of light because their deeds were evil. Everyone who does evil hates the light, and will not come into the light for fear that their deeds will be exposed. But whoever lives by the truth comes into the light, so that it may be seen plainly that what they have done has been done in the sight of God." (NIV)

Notice how Jesus paints the picture of repentance here. Coming into the light means you admit the darkness is sin, and you must decide to step out of it, admitting you are wrong. If you believe in Jesus and choose to follow him, it will mean you choose to step out of living in the darkness of a lie and choose to live in the light of the truth. It is not an apology and continuing to walk in the darkness. It is an apology and turning and walking into the light. Sound impossible? It isn't. The Holy Spirit that fills you when you place your faith in Jesus provides the strength you would have never had to walk in a new direction.

After going to the very beginning of life, to creation, it is determined that the starting point to life itself is relationship with God. He is the Creator of the universe who wills his creation to live in the pursuit of purity and joy while in relationship with him. If we are walking and talking with him, we will start to see his grace being poured out all over our lives. It is through his grace we can see he is a God fueled by his love for us, and I would hope we do not hold back our gratitude.

He is our shepherd, looking out for us always, no matter the circumstances we find ourselves in, and he is the perfect father who will help us become the fathers he designed us to be.

What can we practically do with this information? Well, first, we must not get discouraged. We will never be God and never be perfect, and that is okay. To acknowledge this is the first step. This allows for God's grace to take the lead in our parenting. Even though we are earthly fathers, we get to allow our perfect Father in on our journey and take the lead. It is him and us at the helm of the ship of life, and that is a good place to be.

His leadership of grace and love will guide us and help us navigate life's most intense, confusing, and saddening moments. Pay attention to him and learn from him and his example. We have the template of a perfect Father at our fingertips. Let's lean into it.

With God in the lead, this leaves us under his wing. Who are we thought to be next to God, and why would he let us just go about it with his guidance, whether we listen or not? This is a good question, and to answer it, it will take more than a few sentences. Let us dive into who we are in the next chapter.

CHAPTER 2

We Are Masterpieces

M ozart, Michelangelo, Beethoven, Bach, da Vinci, van Gogh—the list goes on. Even if you are not a person who enjoys the fine arts, chances are you have heard of at least one of these names. What do they have in common besides being fine artists? These individuals all created masterpieces, and their legacies live on through their creations. You are probably thinking, "What do these old dudes who created masterpieces have to do with me?" Well, to be honest, maybe nothing, but I need your mind to be thinking about creators and their masterpieces.

These incredible masters of their art did not create their masterpieces overnight. It took time. Greatness cannot be completed overnight. There must be a willingness to spend time with your artwork to shape it, mold it, or form it into what is envisioned. One cannot just spend a little time here and a little time there. A masterpiece comes about when one has a consistent rhythm forged from the discipline of the will. Over time with this dedicated effort, these artists brought forth work that the world knows to this day.

Before you continue reading, answer this question to yourself. Have you ever stopped to think about who you are? In chapter 1, we covered the importance of God and how he is the greatest father and our starting point. Here in chapter 2, we will examine us, who we are, and the life we are called to. Let us begin with the following verses for some context.

- Ephesians 2:10: "For we are God's masterpiece. He has created us anew in Christ Jesus, so we can do the good things he planned for us long ago."
- Philippians 1:6: "And I am certain that God, who began the good work within you, will continue his work until it is finally finished on the day when Christ Jesus returns."

If you are not following, let me connect some dots here. Instead of a great artist from long ago, we have an eternal God who is creating masterpieces—you, us. However, we are not yet finished masterpieces, but works in progress.

This information leaves us a choice and, I would even say, hope. For the rest of our lives, we get to choose to become masterpieces if we wish. Have you tried creating what you thought you should look like? Are you struggling with bad habits or shame about who you are? Not happy with decisions that have landed you in a situation that seems like a dead end? Feeling depressed like you ruined everything God had planned for you? This is not the end!

Just like the artists who spent consistent time with their creations in order for them to become masterpieces, we get this opportunity with God. He is eager to continue molding, shaping, and creating us to become the masterpieces he had in mind from the beginning. Even though he is eager, we must decide to meet with him to let him do his work. Spending consistent time with the Lord is the way to let him continue his work with us. He can take the blemishes we have had done to us or done to ourselves and repurpose those into his beautiful masterpieces. After all, he is a God of resurrection and renewal. There is nothing we can do to ruin the plan of the masterpiece he has envisioned for us.

As the verses we read earlier explained, one day, we will be brought to completion. However, how much we are willing to be shaped and created here on earth is up to us. How often are we intentionally spending quality time with our Creator? When was the last time you just went on a walk and talked with God? We can see that the relationships we currently have take intentionality to develop, and it is no different for our relationship with God. As life progresses, I encourage you to start being more intentional in your relationship with Jesus. Give him more of your time so he can continue doing his work, changing your life, and creating you as he desires.

I will not spend a lot of time on this topic, but letting God work on us won't feel good. Picture yourself as the statue of David as the original marble slab. Michelangelo just started hitting and chiseling away everything that was not the statue; it couldn't have felt good. So do not be discouraged if you are spending time with God and life seems to be getting painful. It is only everything that is not you that God is chiseling away.

If we are willing to let God continue creating us as masterpieces, the next step is to start walking in the calling he has for us. He will be changing us daily, so our path is not going to be clear, but our steps will be. The Bible explains that his Word is a lamp for our feet and a light to our path. Lamps only allow you to see the next few steps, not the whole path. There is going to be a purpose behind every step. Our path is not going to be fully known, but we will be discovering our purpose with each step. We can be confident that every step will be taken with purpose. Knowing that the end of the path is being with Jesus for eternity gives us strength, encouragement, and hope to continue walking. The farther you walk, the clearer your path becomes.

So let's start taking steps with purpose. Let's pause and break this down. What is the purpose of our steps? You may be thinking, "How do I even know my purpose, much less walk in it?" We are about to go full circle. Hang with me one more moment!

In 1 Samuel 16, we read the story of Samuel searching for the next king of Israel that God had in mind. Samuel saw strong, tall, and handsome men but was confused when God did not select them as the next king. God then spoke to Samuel: "But the Lord said to Samuel, 'Don't judge by his appearance or height, for I have rejected him. The Lord doesn't see things the way you see them. People judge by outward appearance, but the Lord looks at the heart'" (1 Sam. 16:7).

Here is the full circle, a heart after God is led to purpose. A heart after God is someone who is consistently spending time with God, getting to know him, and letting God do his work on your life. Remember in chapter 1, how I stated that none of this is our own work and God does it all? When we have our hearts after God, he leads our feet to their next steps. One can feel the purpose behind every step as our feet hit the ground. This is how we stay on the path he has in mind for us. If he is placing our feet, then we never need to fear walking off the path, ruining the plan, or missing the purpose for our lives. This is all supernaturally done through our hearts in consistent pursuit of God.

More simply put, a heart after God is someone who longs and desires to consistently be in the presence of God. It is through time spent with God that we are led, step by step, with purpose along the path planned for us to walk. As we walk, we are becoming the masterpieces God designed us to be. When we reach the end of our life here on earth, we will be the perfect masterpiece he had designed, and we will be walking into the arms of Jesus, hearing the words "Welcome home, son. I love you, and I am so proud of you!"

Continuing the conversation, we are going to start discussing whom we will become and what life will start looking like as masterpieces of God. Although God is in the business of changing your life, you must be willing to put your skin in the game, or you cannot expect to see results. God never forces you to do something new; that will always be your choice. Keep this in mind as we finish up this chapter. God will provide the change and ability to do so, but we must choose to live out of the power he provides.

Trusting God with the tools and talents we have is vital to our becoming. It is easy to compare ourselves to others and think we have nothing to offer or are missing the mark, or to doubt our potential. Here is an example from the story of David and Goliath found in the book of 1 Samuel in the Bible:

> When the story begins, it emphasizes how small and insignificant David is. His brothers are soldiers in the army, but he, the youngest, is still just a shepherd at home. He is sent to bring cheese sandwiches to his older brothers in the army as it faces off against the Philistines. And when he gets to the camp, he discovers that the

whole army is paralyzed with fear of one Philistine fighter, a giant named Goliath.

David volunteers to fight Goliath, which is crazy. But David figures he has fought lions and bears as a shepherd, so he can fight Goliath. So the army suits him up with armor, but it is too big for him to even walk in. David goes to fight Goliath with a sling and five smooth stones, the weapons of a shepherd boy.

He wins, and Goliath is slain, and little David is a hero.[1]

In this story, David did not argue or compare his choice of weapon to take down the giant. He was content using the tools God had provided him and what he was well versed in. When David went to fight Goliath, he looked down and saw five smooth stones. David knew a sling and those stones were the tool necessary to take down the giant. He did not overthink the circumstance, question his abilities, or doubt his talent. He had trust. David trusted God and the tools he provided him to accomplish the task at hand.

The same applies to us. The gifts and talents we have from God are given for what he has in mind for us. Do not pick up a body suit of armor and sword when God built you to fight with the sling and stones.

"Comparison kills calling," said Shawn Johnson. This quote nails why we have no business letting ourselves get caught up in the comparison game. For example, I often

---

[1] "Leader Resource 1: David and Goliath Background Information," Unitarian Universalist Association, uua.org, accessed December 9, 2024, https://www.uua.org/re/tapestry/multigenerational/hebrewscriptures/workshop1/188980.shtml.

compare myself with other dads. I compare how they interact with their kids, the things they buy for them, how they maintain their hobbies, and what their strengths and talents are, and the list goes on. Am I the only one? I have come to notice, in my comparison, that I am only comparing (1) what I feel insecure about, (2) what I have chosen to lay down or sacrifice for what I believe God has called me to pursue, or (3) what I do not have. If I get caught up in comparing myself, I slowly start killing my focus on the calling I know God has set before me, ignoring gratitude for how he made me, and I start trying to attain what is not meant for me.

Celebrate what someone else is called to instead of comparing. Uniquely made, we are all created for different purposes.

In 2 Timothy 1:9, it states, "For God saved us and called us to live a holy life. He did this, not because we deserved it, but because that was his plan from before the beginning of time—to show us his grace through Christ Jesus."

Since we are done comparing ourselves to others, let us focus on what God has in mind for our lives to look like. As this Scripture shares, our lives are supposed to look holy. Holy simply means "set apart" at its basic definition. This is an aspect of God's will for us. Our lives are to be set apart from society. Think about the character of Jesus all through the Bible. He conducted himself in a way that was very set apart from everyone. Everyone knew there was something different about Jesus after encounters with him.

In the Sermon on the Mount, Jesus explains we should be the salt of the earth and the light of the world. If you want to do some more background reading on this story, the story can be found in Matthew 5:13–16. You cannot hide the presence of salt in a meal, and wherever there is light, darkness cannot exist. Our presence in society should be noticed, not because we have Jesus in our hearts and act like the world, but because we have Jesus in our hearts and stand out apart from the world. We are not to just be noticed but also felt.

What does standing out like salt and light look like? Looking like Jesus to others is the goal. This is why it is very important to be spending time with God, as we covered earlier. In order to live and become like someone, you have to spend time with that someone. If we do not know that Jesus was for truth over lying, for example, we would not be aware that we should start telling the truth. (It's an obvious example, I know, but I wanted to paint the picture.)

What about a more practical example? As I have gotten to know Jesus, I have discovered his patience. This has challenged my response to my children when they push every button in my body. I fail a lot, but I also am so much more aware and praying for the strength to be patient. It is easy to lash out in anger and snap at my kids, but it takes self-control to have patience. When the family and others see patience as a response over anger, it reflects to the world something different. It reflects the character of Jesus.

When society sees us, they should see Jesus reflected through our behaviors and actions. We get a choice to live differently, but the strength to do this is not on our own. The strength is because of the power of the Holy Spirit within us. Do not forget this; it is extremely important. God does the work to change us, but we get to choose to live differently.

My challenge to us all is to think and read about Jesus and his life. This is a good way to start discovering his character. I am going to share a list of questions that I thought of as I started reading the Bible to get to know Jesus that were deeply challenging to what I believed. Each question was a moment

23

in my life when I was stuck at a crossroads, having to decide between believing what I just discovered in the Bible about Jesus and what I grew up with.

- Did Jesus follow an authority for his life (family, governments, and so forth)?
- Did Jesus obey in all circumstances?
- Did Jesus waver in what was right for what was culturally accepted?
- Did Jesus choose love over hate for people who deserved it?
- Did Jesus swear?
- Did Jesus talk down about people, either to their faces or when they were not in the room?
- Did Jesus tell racist, crude, or inappropriate jokes for the sake of a laugh in the room?
- Did Jesus abuse substances?
- Did Jesus manipulate others for self-gain?
- Did Jesus have contempt in his heart or mind for others?
- Did Jesus judge those he thought he knew better than?
- Did Jesus stand up for those who needed defending?
- Did Jesus run over people with truth or stand aside offering grace?
- Did Jesus shy away from bringing glory to his Father when it was uncomfortable?
- Did Jesus (fill in your own question here) _____?

I will not share any answers God and I arrived at for these questions. To be transparent, I am still wrestling with all these. Wrestling looks like deciding whether I want to apply to my life what I believe God has revealed to me. Also, some of these questions I still have no answer for and am still pursuing for God to show me.

What happens if we start adjusting our lives to become like Jesus? I believe we start affecting everyone around us in a positive, "God kind" of way. Imagine if your wife, kids, and all your relationships interacted with you and walked away feeling like they knew about who Jesus was a little bit more because of you. The world is hurting for more Christians to stop telling people how to live and start showing people what a changed life looks like. Stop it with the "cool Christians." You know what I mean. If actions speak louder than words, why are we always quick to tell people about Jesus with our words instead of our actions?

What does this mean for us as fathers? It looks like having a devoted relationship with Jesus, being fathers after the Father's heart. Our character will begin to be shaped and molded into that of Christ, and we will start to take on the template of the greatest Father. Imagine looking a bit like God in your parenting. This is a dream of mine. Even though it is impossible to be perfect and I am not about to start trying to be, I desire to embrace the template of fatherhood God has established. Since I cannot muster up enough strength to put it on myself, I want to spend time with the One who can.

All right, we covered a lot in this chapter. We discussed being God's masterpieces, being men after God's own heart, and the lives we could be choosing to live. My hope was to shed new light on the fact that life change is not from us but from spending time in the presence of God, our Creator.

While becoming his masterpieces, we also get to choose to live as those masterpieces. Since God will not force us to live differently, we get the amazing privilege of free will to decide for ourselves. Galatians 5:13 says, "For you have been called to live in freedom, my brothers and sisters. But don't use your freedom to satisfy your sinful nature. Instead, use your freedom to serve one another in love." There are two options on the table: living how we always have, or living the life of the masterpiece that will change the world for generations to come.

When we choose to live out of the place of becoming the masterpieces we were designed to be, we can have confidence in our decisions and the direction in which we are steering the ship of fatherhood. If we are spending time with God, we will be hearing, seeing, and knowing how he would direct the ship. Even though we will make mistakes along the way, it is nice to know we can learn what to do.

Why does this matter? Well for one reason, our children will be the greatest beneficiaries. Kids, as we know, are anything but normally functioning humans. Let me share two quick stories from personal experience to explain. But first, be prepared; this first one is going to be a poop story.

When James was eleven months old or so, my wife and I were cleaning the house, and he was in his playpen area, having a grand old time. My wife soon started looking curiously at James, and I could tell from the look in her eyes, she was asking a perplexing question to herself. Before I could analyze the situation further, her shriek of "Ewwww!" flooded the house!

I quickly hurried over to the commotion and quickly realized what had become of my wife. She discovered that James created his own type of Play-Doh . . . his poop. James was rubbing it all up and down the bars of the playpen and was about to stick his hand in his mouth before my wife jumped in to remedy the situation!

On a less nasty note, my daughter June had a unique story of her own. She wants to always be like her older brother. One day when we were dropping James off at school, my wife walked him and June into the school to the assembly area. In this area, all the grades gathered together for the morning and sat grouped together from youngest to the oldest. This school also watched young toddlers who were June's age.

When the morning activities were over, each class was dismissed, one at a time. When the young toddlers were dismissed, June got up and started walking away with them. She just naturally assumed that she must go with the other kids of her size and stature. It was cute and silly to see her independently think she knew what she was supposed to do.

Kids are interesting, aren't they—from lack of bowel control to just doing whatever they think they should? How do we even begin to help the crazy, cute, and cuddly creatures? Well, to really understand children, continue with me in the next chapter.

CHAPTER 3

Who Made You a Father?

"**B**utt crack, praise the Lord! Butt crack, praise the Lord!" James shouted as he was dancing around the house without his pants. As he was doing this, I thought, "The toddler years are interesting, aren't they?" Toddlers are tiny humans with no filters and little understanding. Often messy and gross, kids are also extremely adorable at the same time. Hearing these exclamations throughout the house brought my heart joy and was such a blessing to hear, even as weird as it was!

In this chapter, we get to work through what—or rather, who—made you a father in the first place: your children. As I mentioned previously, my son James is only four, my daughter June is two, and little Jovi is our newest member of the family. I am still discovering every day more and more about who and what children are, and I have many years ahead in regard to this topic. But for the premise of this book, I have learned enough for the foundational and beginning years.

I am going to ask and answer three questions in this chapter that I have found to be key and pivotal in understanding children. First, to whom do our children belong? Second, why are they considered blessings? Third, what do they need for survival?

At the end of this chapter, I will tie these answers together to make sense of how they are related. I do warn you, this chapter may seem disjointed or have an odd flow, but please stick it out. I promise it will all make sense at the end.

Question One: To Whom Do Our Children Belong?

Interestingly, the most important piece of advice I would give to any dad is also the most basic. Here it is: your kids are not yours. Your children are God's children. As I was looking into this, I discovered that from inception, God created us with our souls.

Ezekiel 18:4 states: "Behold, all souls are Mine; The soul of the father as well as the soul of the son is Mine" (NKJV). Here God lays out the fact that everyone is his. This means that when you have a child, you are actually given a soul to take care of and raise, given to you by God.

Ecclesiastes 12:7 states, "And the dust returns to the ground it came from, and the Spirit returns to God who gave it" (NIV).

Have you ever thought of it this way before? Up until recently, I have not. It is not something to blink and move past quickly. This is perhaps the largest and most important foundational truth about kids, and we must take time to understand this to fully recognize our role as fathers. God entrusted us to take care of, raise, teach, and shepherd his children.

To answer question one, our children are the Lord's and are given by him.

Question Two: Why Are Children Considered Blessings?

"Children are a gift from the Lord; they are a reward from him. Children born to a young man are like arrows in a warrior's hands. How joyful is the man whose quiver is full of them! He will not be put to shame when he confronts his accusers at the city gates" (Ps. 127:3–5).

This is the popular verse where I think we get the idea of children being gifts. I want to actually take a moment to think about this instead of just taking it word for word. Since children are given to us, children are technically gifts from God. How are we stewarding this gift? To "steward" means to be trusted with responsibility over something that is not yours. Stewarding souls from God—is this the definition of being a father you had in mind?

When we receive a gift, we are blessed. Therefore, we can conclude children, gifts from the Lord, are blessings.

I find this interesting. A gift is a blessing, and children are given to be blessings. God wants to bless you in ways you can never know, and I think he does this through our children. Sadly, I do not think we give this much thought. I cannot tell you how many times I stop and stare and take in so many amazing moments with my children. All I can think about when James says things in an adorable way or when my daughters do something cute is "Wow, I am so blessed." My children and wife are the main sources in my life that constantly remind me I am blessed.

Remember getting socks or underwear as a kid and the disappointment that brought at Christmas or your birthday? Feelings of despair fill your heart? Sadly, this is what people have been turning having kids into: lame gifts. Satan has infiltrated culture to have an opposite take on children if you have recently noticed this. Even in Christian subcultures, we find many people with views of children as burdens, weights, or simply disappointments. This is the 180-degree opposite of what God says about the matter.

Some things to keep in mind: You may be reading this book and struggling with infertility. Please do not think God does not want to bless you because you cannot have kids. I would encourage all of us to hold out our hands to receive willingly. Giving birth to your own children is not the only way God bestows these gifts. I was adopted. My parents, the ones who adopted me, struggled with having kids of their own, and God gave them me and two other wonderful children. They kept their hands open, expectant, and willing to receive the way God wanted to give his gift of blessing.

To answer question number two, our children are considered blessings because they are gifts from God

Question Three: What Do They Need for Survival?

On May 20, 2020, I was about two months into being a dad for the first time to James. I journaled the following:

> Creating things from matter requires energy that we have, and it is what makes us to be created in God's image and likeness. Only God can create matter from nothing, but we can create matter from matter. God is the ultimate energy, and this is how he can create something from nothing. [Some of us] can even create people. Having a baby and raising a child is creating a person. God created humans, and we can make more.

This is weird to grasp; we are like God but definitely not God. (Pause: God has control of all things; we do not. Please do not think I am saying we are God by any means; we just have similarities. After all, we are made in his image.)

Does this change how we work? Parent? Genesis 1 says we have dominion and use our energy and mind to create and for the earth. Work is a version of taking matter that we have access to and turning it into something else. Baking a cake takes multiple forms of matter and transforms it into one piece of completely different matter. You created something.

In parenting, we are creating a person. The child is dependent on you to show it how to be human.

I think that the last sentence of this journal entry is missing a vital piece of information. God is the ultimate Creator, and one of the ways that we are invited to join in and participate in his world is through the raising of children.

The first part of this journal entry breaks down our ability to create. When we have a child, we create a new person. God supplied life and soul, but he gave us the ability to create the body. Unlike a cake, once this baby is born, that is not the end of the creation process but rather the beginning. This child will be completely dependent on you to show it how to be human, survive, learn, love, grow, and so on.

Teaching, training, and developing will be the responsibilities we carry with this creation. Your teaching and training must be rooted in the truth of God's Word. What your child needs for survival is to know how to be human. If you want your child to know how to be human, they must know the story of humanity, and that can only be found in the Bible from page 1 to the end.

To answer question three, your child needs your teaching and training for their survival. It is imperative to be rooted in God's Word, as he is the only source of truth.

All right, we covered all of the questions, which in all honestly probably only brought on more questions. Please wrestle with whatever questions come to mind, and I urge you to write them down in the margins of this book before you forget. But if you are like me, you do not have a pen while reading, so let's continue and tie these questions all together.

To recap, our three answers to the questions are:

1) Our children are created by the Lord and are his.

2) Our children are considered blessings because they are gifts from God.

3) Our children need teaching and training for their survival.

God created human beings and filled them with souls. They come into the earth in the form of babies that are in need of nurturing, love, and care. As time goes on, teaching and training become imperative for their survival in this world. But that is not all children are. Somehow, in a Godlike way that I will never understand on this side of heaven, despite all the work kids seem to be, one's heart could not be more full when teaching and training children in the truth of their existence. They are the truest form of a blessing I have ever experienced (next to my spouse, but that will be another book). Having blessings does not mean there will be no heartbreak or pain. Remember, we live in a broken world. But take in the moments where you just feel blessed.

Can I provide a challenge to you as I have to myself already? Dad, you are responsible for teaching and training the soul(s) God entrusted to you in the truth of him and his world he created. Steward this gift wisely.

In light of this challenge to you, I hope you can see why I started the book the way I did. Because culture has a different view of God, us, and even our children, it is important to understand these entities according to the Word of God. Once we get to our children, we notice our relationship with God becomes the focal point of fatherhood. God is the foundation of the world, our lives, and our children's lives. We cannot teach and train in what we do not have. It is never too late to start teaching and training yourself in God's truth. Start now.

How do we make an impact on our children's souls? It takes time and intentionality. We will talk about time a little later in this book, so let's focus on being intentional. We can achieve great success and wealth, but if we ignore our kids, what is it all for?

As I had to make a choice when my son was born, we all get to make a choice every day where we will choose to be intentional. James, June, and Jovi will need a father who is intent on doing the little things for them. The same goes for your children. If we will not do the little things like change a diaper, swaddle our young one, or sit down and play with them, why would we think we can be intentional with the large things in their life? Here is a little bit of wisdom. In order to have the relationship for those hard midnight kitchen-counter conversations, there has to be trust. Trust is developed over time. Changing diapers and doing the little things through the infant and toddler years develops in your child a sense of trust. These are little things to you, but very big things to them. As time goes on, these little frequent tasks will turn into larger and not-as-often ones. Are we willing to be prepared? God teaches in his Word, faithful in little, faithful in much.

Being there for their everyday needs now will have a profound impact on being there for their everyday needs later. It will cultivate a lush environment to shepherd their souls, as they will trust what you teach because you practice what you preach. Teaching and training must be backed up by action. Put down the beer and change the diaper, leave the TV for a moment to help your kid when they are crying from an injury, and be tender to their emotions when they are having a nighttime meltdown. These are not tasks to be saved exclusively for the wife; these are for you as well.

Having covered God, us, and our children, this chapter concludes the "cast" section of this book. We must train and teach our gifts from God, and the most effective way is through our actions. Start now, wherever you are at in this journey, taking one step at a time with the little things. I promise it will make a difference. Think about hiking: One does not get to the destination without first taking little steps to get started.

Speaking of which, who even likes hiking? Well, I hate it, for one. Except that there is a certain type of trail that I enjoy. It is one that leads to a body of water, like a lake, pond, or river. One of my favorite places I have ever been to was Hanging Lake in Colorado—a grueling hike with the greatest reward.

Coincidentally enough, most of these lakes located on the tops of mountains have beautiful, majestic, and awe-inspiring waterfalls feeding them. I could lose myself for hours staring at the water fall over the edge and crash elegantly, yet ferociously, into the water below.

Relationships are like a waterfall. Curious as to how? Well, join me in the next section of this book as we continue on our journey through the foundation of fatherhood.

PART 2

PRIORITY MANAGEMENT

CHAPTER 4

The Relationship
Waterfall: Priorities

What does everyone get but also stops for no one? Time. This terrible riddle, if we can even call it that, is what this chapter is all about. In the upcoming chapters, we will look at how time plays perhaps the most important role in our lives. It is something we never get back. Time to take it seriously (pun fully intended).

Ever show up to your friends or family the day after they have a party, event, or get-together that you did not attend? Usually, we are met with "Where were you?" or "Why don't you make time for your favorite people?" or "How come you didn't want to see us yesterday?" Hopefully, these comments are all out of love, but sometimes it can also feel like there is a hidden message in these words about how they should have been the priority. This word, priority, gets tossed around a lot, so let us define our term for this chapter. What is a priority?

A priority is something that is valued or treated as more important than something else. For example, which would take a higher priority in your life: bingeing the new season of your favorite TV show or taking out the trash that is only half full? Easy: I would pick the show. Most of us probably value entertainment and relaxation over working, especially if that work is something hard and dirty.

All right, let's think through another scenario. You made plans to hang out with the guys and your car has a flat tire. A little trickier? Knowing the ingenuity of man, you would find a way to hang out with the guys while fixing the flat. So this one could go either way, depending on you and what you value.

Let's try an even tougher one.

Your family or close friend group has made plans to celebrate a once-in-a-while event for someone in it, like a graduation from college, a going-away party, or special event of some sort. Either way, this is one you do not want to miss. You RSVP'd yes, and the wife and kids are ecstatic for it!

The morning of the event, your wife wakes up dealing with a lot of stress, anxiety, depression, or [fill in the blank]. After talking, you can tell that this get-together will be too much for her, and she even stated that it might be too much. However, being the sweet soul that your wife is, she mentions that she doesn't want to ruin the fun and the family should still go. What do you do? Whom do you prioritize? Oh, I forgot to mention, your kids are also chirping at you like little birds about how excited they are to go.

How would you even decide this one? Do you prioritize all the people and the event, your spouse, or your kids?

I hope you are beginning to see the importance of priorities. In this American culture, I see mass confusion around what priorities should be. I sense that they do not exist or we have two foundational ones, like family and work. Life becomes a mess when we do not have the right priorities or hold them in the incorrect order.

Time and priorities go hand in hand. We are only given so much time on this earth, and where we spend it and with whom we spend it matters. In this chapter, I want to help you prioritize your time when it comes to the relationships in your life as a father. There are more players on the board, and sometimes it seems too hard to know who should be a priority.

In the world of relationships, I have discovered that there is a strategic order to them, and I call that the relationship waterfall.

Time to dive in. What does it mean that there is a strategic order to relationships? Searching the Bible, I have found there is a waterfall method to the relationships we must prioritize. The waterfall method is where we start at the top, then move to the next one, then the next, and so forth, all the way to the bottom—just like a waterfall. The relationships we should be prioritizing in order are: our relationship with God, ourselves, our spouse, our kids, our extended family, fellow believers, and the unbelievers in our life.

After our relationship with God, these can be divided up into two categories: relationships with those God entrusted to our care and responsibility, and those who are not.

Let me clarify something that I will expand on a bit later in this chapter. As we will see, our relationships with God, ourselves, our spouse, and our kids are definitely top of the list. But. Say you have a crazy uncle (extended family) and your best friend is in town (either a believer or unbeliever) at the same time. Whom do you choose? This waterfall would suggest the crazy uncle, and I want to make sure it is known that these last few relationships and who gets priority are a matter of the season of life. The order in which you prioritize these would be dependent on what you are led by God to pursue most at the time for the season of life you are in.

Ready to start diving over the waterfall? Let's go.

1. God

Deuteronomy 6:5–6 states, "And you must love the Lord your God with all your heart, all your soul, and all your strength. And you must commit yourselves wholeheartedly to these commands that I am giving you today."

Mark 12:29–30, we read, "Jesus replied, 'The most important commandment is this: "Listen, O Israel! The Lord our God is the one and only Lord. And you must love the Lord your God with all your heart, all your soul, all your mind, and all your strength."'"

Nothing is more important in life than your relationship with God. He is the Creator of all relationships, so he should be number one. These Scriptures clearly show that our time spent with God needs to come above all else. On the top drop of our relationship waterfall, God resides. We can give God all our heart, soul, mind, and strength when we give him our first. This verse does not say to just give God your heart, soul, mind, and strength. It says give all. It is impossible to give all if we have already given away to other relationships.

This is the core of life: that our priorities allow us and those around us to have a flourishing relationship with God. Life is all about him; how do we leverage ourselves to make that a reality for us and those around us? Continue with me down this waterfall.

2. Ourselves

I am not sure if I am late to the game and most men know to prioritize themselves or if this is breaking news. Either way, something very important to schedule in is taking care of ourselves mentally, physically, spiritually, and emotionally. This will look different for all of us, as what fills us up in these ways will vary from guy to guy.

The reason why this is important is because we have people depending on us, and we need to put our best foot forward for them. It's like the old airplane cliché, "Before assisting your children with their air masks if we lose cabin pressure, set yours up first, then you can help." Don't sacrifice yourself and trick yourself into thinking you will be okay if you are depleted. Put your oxygen mask on first. A piece of caution comes with this priority, though. Don't make yourself an idol. Since it feels good to fill up our cup, it can become too easy to give ourselves too much time and let the other relationships in our lives take a hit. Make sure you are not taking too much time away from the other relationships in your life. Find the balance.

3. Your Spouse

The next level is your spouse, the first relationship that God entrusted to your care. Ephesians 5 sums it up nicely:

> For husbands, this means love your wives, just as Christ loved the church. He gave up his life for her to make her holy and clean, washed by the cleansing of God's word. He did this to present her to himself as a glorious

43

church without a spot or wrinkle or any other blemish. Instead, she will be holy and without fault. In the same way, husbands ought to love their wives as they love their own bodies. For a man who loves his wife actually shows love for himself. No one hates his own body but feeds and cares for it, just as Christ cares for the church. (Eph. 5:25–29)

You may be wondering: How does this Scripture point out this should be the second relationship we prioritize? Well, that is a good question. In this Scripture, we see a comparison to how Christ loved the church and how we love our own bodies.

Christ loves his church so much that he gave his life. There are very few people whom I would give my life for. These people would have to be very close to me and people I care deeply about. Also, it would include people I highly prioritize and value. We know Jesus loves his Father and prioritizes him as number one; we can see this in the way Jesus is always talking and doing his Father's will while on earth.

How much do you love your body? Probably a lot. You care if you get it hurt, you care how it looks, you care that it is healthy, and you think about it daily. Essentially, this writing is saying: Next to your relationship with God, prioritize and value your relationship with your spouse. After all, when you get married, you become one. It almost seems obsessive, but we should be thinking about our wives like we do our own bodies. This paints a clear picture that a spouse takes relationship priority number two.

Argue with me for a moment. "Steven, I have babies and toddlers, and they require way more than my spouse does. How can I possibly ignore them to spend time with my wife who is self-sustainable?" My response would be that I agree—

almost. What people require and what makes a relationship flourish, I would argue, are different. Flourishing relationships take communication and intentionality. Take care of your kids, do not ignore them, but think about how you will be intentional to create a space to build a blossoming relationship with your spouse. Hint: You will have to say no to a lot of loud voices competing for your time. Remember, your kids will eventually grow up and move out. It will then be you and your spouse. How do you want that relationship to look and feel, come that time of being an empty nester?

4. Your Children

This segues nicely to the other relationships within our realm of responsibility: our children. God, your spouse, and your children—the big three. Earlier in this book, we looked at how children are gifts from God that we are to steward wisely. Ephesians backs up this claim: "Fathers, do not be too hard on your children so they will become angry. Bring them up in the training and instruction of the Lord" (Eph. 6:4 NLV/NIV).

Paul is writing to be gentle with our children, raising them with teaching and training; we quickly see that this requires a lot of our time. This is a full-time job, and that is why kids are often the easiest distraction to misalign the relational priorities in our lives. Since we just debunked the common lie that our children are more important than our spouses, we do not have to spend a lot of bandwidth figuring out that they come next. Teaching and training our children will take intentionality to keep them as a priority.

5. Those Not Entrusted to Your Care

These last three relationships in the waterfall lie in the realm of those God has not placed in your direct care and responsibility. The order in which you prioritize these is dependent on what you are led by God to pursue most at the time and season of life you are in. Spend a lot of time in prayer, and ask for God's guidance on these relationships. These relationships are non-Jesus-follower friendships, extended family, and church/Jesus-follower friendships.

A. Nonbelievers

Matthew 28:18–20 states: "Jesus came and told his disciples, 'I have been given all authority in heaven and on earth. Therefore, go and make disciples of all the nations, baptizing them in the name of the Father and the Son and the Holy Spirit. Teach these new disciples to obey all the commands I have given you. And be sure of this: I am with you always, even to the end of the age.'"

To help discover who we should be prioritizing after the people who are placed into our care and responsibility, we can ask ourselves a question: Whom can we disciple? In case you missed it, Jesus says, "Go and make disciples." He does not say, "Go and tell people about me and baptize them, then move on to someone else." Our priority is to spend time with the few in our lives who are open and able to learn from us about the commands he has given us. Simply put, discipleship is helping people follow Jesus.[2] This may mean helping people who are already following Jesus or helping people who are not yet following him. It is not just a word that applies to Christians.

If you are anything like me as an adult, and especially an adult with young kids, we seem to have no time. This is why I absolutely love this passage from Jesus because he takes the pressure off needing to be everything to everyone. We as parents have the ability to disciple the few with our limited time, and that is okay. A lot of churches today focus on the mission of telling many people about Jesus, and I absolutely love that. But because of this, I have personally felt very guilty for the last few years about not spreading the gospel and discipling every person I meet.

Because my time to spend with those outside my family went down due to new relationships in my family, I felt like I was not doing what Jesus commanded of me; I spend the majority of my time around my family and believers only. But I realized three things: (1) I am discipling my children, who are, in fact, at this point in time, nonbelievers (more on this in a moment); (2) I can still engage with my existing friends and neighbors, believers or not; and (3) I do get the opportunity to share Jesus with anyone I meet on any given day, which is also an opportunity to show our kids "faith in action."

Before I continue, I want to address "children as nonbelievers." I am not saying that if our children at any point tragically pass, they are not going to heaven for being unbelievers. I am recognizing that our children, until they are

---

2   Christina M Embree, "What Does It Mean 'To Disciple' Our Kids?" Refocus, refocusministry.org, January 23, 2024, https://refocusministry.org/what-does-it-mean-to-disciple-our-kids/.

at an age of understanding, have not made a conscious decision to be "believers." My two-year-old daughter, for example, can barely say full sentences, much less grasp the concepts of sin, grace, and salvation through faith in Jesus. This is a much deeper topic, but I believe God takes care of our children, should tragedy strike. I know the Bible provides guidance on this topic, and I encourage you to read and seek the wisdom of those who understand this topic more theologically in depth if you are interested in learning more.

Back to the believers' three things I learned.

These three points of view taught me that I do not have to feel guilty anymore, but I still need to be intentional. Our commission as followers of Jesus is to make disciples through discipleship. We do not need to be focused on many individuals and their conversion, but instead, we can focus on the few in our circle and their discipleship. After all, it is through discipleship that people will learn what it is to follow Jesus on their own and hopefully make that decision one day for themselves. This helps narrow down the crowd of potential relationships outside our realm of responsibility to a select few, those we disciple and those who disciple us.

What about the family and fellowship relationships? Where do these work themselves in the waterfall? I am glad you asked.

B. Extended Family

In 1 Timothy 5:8, Paul writes that those who neglect to take care of their own family are often worse than unbelievers. Something I never knew about this was the context in which it was written. Paul was writing about financially taking care of people in the church. When he writes this statement, my research shows it was referring to not just your home, but also to your extended home and family connections. Since money is such a strong indicator of where our values lie, it shows here that we must value our extended family relationships, not just the ones under our own roof. In the case of Paul's letter, it was through financial means to support family, but I believe we must look at this with a broader lens. Time, talent, and treasure. Where can we help with any of these?

C. Fellow Believers

Hebrews 10:24–25 is about Christians not giving up on meeting together and actually encourages it. This is seen in most modern-day churches. We gather weekly at a service surrounded by fellow believers. Perhaps you are in a small group or meet consistently with friends who share the faith. This is key; we need relationships like this to be encouraged, challenged, and inspired in the faith. Proverbs 27 tells us that as iron sharpens iron, so one person will sharpen another. We need discipleship. Navigating life with others who share the faith makes life much easier to get through. We all disciple each other. When you are in a pickle, you have people you can talk to. They may not be theologians, but you know they have your best interest in mind, share the same pursuit of Jesus in their lives, and want to help you follow him.

It is refreshing to have these relationships. In those moments when we are going through challenging situations as dads, we need to have other men in our life whom we can share a burden with, rejoice with, or just enjoy the refreshment that other like-minded beings bring to our lives. There is a verse in the Bible that states "The generous will prosper, those who refresh others, will themselves be refreshed" (Proverbs 11:25). Do you need a breath of fresh air in your life? Make an effort to start developing these relationships.

You may have friends in your life who do not share the faith of following Jesus. That is okay, and it is still important to spend time with them. They will not be people in your life who will be sharpening or refreshing you in your spiritual growth, but they need your discipleship to know who Jesus is so hopefully they make a decision to follow him for themselves.

Phew, that was a lot of relationships to cover, but we did it! Let's review for a moment. When we combine the strategic order of relationships with discipleship, it helps provide clarity on relationships we should be prioritizing. We start with the relationships God has given us direct responsibility over, then we work our way outward from there. Asking ourselves, "Whom can we disciple?" and praying about it helps guide us to those in our current season of life we should be prioritizing.

So here are a couple questions for you.

How are you being discipled? How are you discipling your wife, kids, and those around you? This is why priorities and their order are so important. Life takes effort and energy, and if we are spending it all out of order, then we ourselves, followed by those closest to us and in our care, will suffer first.

Imagine you start today and rearrange your priorities and where you will choose to spend your time. Say you do this better than you have been just a few days a week. What would change in a month, six months, or year? Would there be a difference in your relationship with God? Do you think your wife and you will be closer and more intimately connected spiritually, emotionally, and physically? What about your children? Will you be able to speak into their lives with more trust and authority? It will feel strange at first, and your family might even be like, "What is Dad doing? Isn't the game on?" or "Why isn't he out with his friends again?" Don't let thoughts like that stop you! Push through the comments or the awkwardness and keep on. Perhaps you even talk self-doubt to yourself like I do. So to that, I say, "Silencio, Bruno!" as Alberto from the movie Luca would say. (If you have not watched that movie yet with your kids, it's only a matter of time.)

Your family and your relationships are worth so much more than you may give them credit for. Fight for what you love. Fighting against Satan trying to steal your time away from what matters is a war we will have to endure our whole lives, but winning one battle at a time is all it takes before we win the war. Christ has won the war, so there is hope we can win the battles with him.

It is easy to take this information we just learned and store it in our heads, but I want to help move the information we just learned to our hands and put it into practice. In the next chapter, we get practical. We take this order of relationships and break it down into what it could possibly look like in our day-to-day routines.

CHAPTER 5

Thrive, Don't Just Survive: Routines

We all have routines. From the moment we wake up to when our head hits the pillow at night, we all follow routines that we set for ourselves. This could be as detailed as brushing your teeth at 5:55 a.m. right when you wake up, or it could be a little more broad, like "Wake up, get ready, head to work." An order that we stick to on a regular basis is a routine. Routines can be complex and require a lot of discipline, or they can be easy and mindless.

For example, most of you have probably come across personal trainers, life coaches, or health enthusiasts who advertise the perfect daily routine on social media. They lay out hour by hour what you need to be doing to achieve success, weight loss, or a happier life. These routines are complex and require a ton of discipline. I do not see advertisements for routines of being a couch potato while bingeing Netflix that bring about desired results. Routines that require convenience and ease are almost like second nature.

of a kiss because (1) it is easy to remember, (2) it is a good physical action to bring you into proximity with her, and (3) it provides a nice segue to engage in any physical, spiritual, or emotional connection.

Something to consider: If our relationship with God is our number one priority, it should be our spouse's top priority as well. I mean this in a humanity type of way. Everyone who places their faith in Jesus should ultimately elevate that relationship to number one on their daily priority list. However, I am not naïve, and I understand not all spouses are believers. If that is where you are in life, I encourage you with this verse from 1 Corinthians 7:14: "For the unbelieving husband has been sanctified through his wife, and the unbelieving wife has been sanctified through her believing husband. Otherwise your children would be unclean, but as it is, they are holy" (NIV).

There is something special in a family where the Lord is. Pray for your spouse and seek the wise counsel of pastors or credible resources for diving deeper into what Paul is writing here.

You see, leading your wife is not about having the job that brings in the money, having all the answers, or being treated like a king. Leading your wife is about creating the space for her to have her relationship with God prioritized. When we and our wives put our relationship with God as number one, everything else in life flows from it. We need to enable our wives to have the best possible relationship with God. It is on them to work the relationship, but we can help daily by creating space and time for them to go meet with God.

After our wives have their time with God, they need time with us. When we got married, we both became one. If we continue walking our separate lives, how is that oneness? I know work is demanding and we have things to do, but our wives should never feel second to those things. If they do, that is a sign that our priorities are out of line and we need to shift things around or make some major changes. Ask yourself this question daily: What does my wife need from me? This will help us keep our wives as a priority.

Pitter-patter, pitter-patter. It is the sound of little feet running down the hall. The kids are up! Morning snuggles, hugs, and kisses are on the way. Like our wives, our kids need our time too.

How we give our time to our children will affect how they think God gives them time. If you are not prioritizing them, they will feel it. They will think God has more important things to do than spend time with them as they grow, even if you tell them that is not the case. How? Actions speak louder than words. If your job takes you away from your kids, put your two weeks' notice in tomorrow and cut back. I do not care how much money it brings in; God provides and takes care of your family. Neglecting our children due to a demanding job is culturally acceptable, but I cannot find in God's Word where he agrees with it. They are his children, as we have already learned, and we are entrusted to take care of them, not neglect them.

Before you go and quit a job you actually need, start calling me a jerk, or [fill in the blank], let me ask some questions. Is there a job that you can get that allows you to still put bread on the table, a roof over everyone's heads, and gas in the car but allows you to have more time?

Are your hobbies excessive and taking you away from your family more than you realize? I advocate for alone time and think it is extremely important for dads to have hobbies that they can just be themselves in. I also know that when many men become husbands and fathers, they do not realize that their time spent on those hobbies cannot be the same as they were when they were single. Where can you, for a season, adjust this routine in your life? For when we are focused on passion for the wrong thing, we won't see what gets sacrificed right away, but time will reveal it.

What are some practical ways we can see this play out? While at the breakfast table, it is a good time for me to think about the whole day and what I can sacrifice to help the home. Maybe we need to lower the expectations on our spouse for worldly things like keeping the house clean, making fresh, home-cooked dinner for the family every night, providing for our every need physically and emotionally, and taking care of the kids full-time. Perhaps it's running errands for her and going grocery shopping with the kids instead of being a couch potato, watching your favorite show, or obsessing over your favorite hobby. Maybe it is time to learn how to cook a few more meals so you can take a turn a couple days a week. Perhaps when you get home (or off work for the work-from-home clan), you can hang out with the kids for thirty minutes to give your wife some quality alone time. Plus you get quality time with the kids. Think outside the box about what you can do.

For your children, are you showing and teaching them about Jesus through every moment of their day? Are you doing simple things like praying before every meal, reading the Bible with them, and praying before bedtime? These are a few things I personally do with my kids daily, and I am always on the lookout for new ways from other seasoned fathers. Do your kids know who God is and how important he is by the words you speak, the messages you share, and the way you act? Do your kids need fewer TikTok videos and viral trends and more teaching about why God made the world he did?

This matters because we only get so much time with them day in and day out. If you are like me, most likely the largest part of any daily routine is work. So let's talk about that for a moment.

We have a responsibility to work. God created us to work. After research and thought, I believe there are two types of work: Work that provides income or a means to a living and work that cultivates the garden of your life. Don't worry if this sounds like a lot of work; God makes sure to carve out time for rest.

Now we are headed off to work!

When we go out to earn a living, it is important to realize that our gifts and talents to perform the work are from God. Since this is the case, we can be confident that God is our Provider, and sustaining a family does not fall entirely on our shoulders. Cultivating the garden in your life refers to the work to be done at home. Contrary to popular opinion, the real work of your life begins when you clock out at your job. Your wife, kids, and home need tending too. It's time to work on what has been entrusted to you.

Hopefully, as you are at work, you are performing with integrity and doing your best. No matter what job we are performing, we must realize it is a job and not our identity. It is so easy as men to find our value in what we get paid for and how much we get paid. We can therefore deduct that men tend to determine their value and how much of a man we are based on our financial income. It is not wrong to want to make good money, but if it determines your identity that you "made it" or "proved him or her wrong," then we have some red flags waving, and we need to tend to those.

I know I have struggled with this at my jobs, so I know the battle is real. My antidote? Getting to know God and learning what he says about me and who I am. The more time I spent learning about my true identity, the easier it was to let the messages like "gotta make more money to be a real man" go.

After work (for most of us, that is probably around 5:00 p.m.), we are going to head home, and it will be time to work the garden. I use this phrase to describe everything that is entrusted to your care. This includes your home, family, or anything where responsibility for care falls under your domain. You're exhausted when you get home, I bet, but does the work stop? Sadly, no. We have to tend the garden, or just like a real garden, weeds will sprout, the good plants will suffer, and our garden will look like a chaotic mess. How do we keep the garden from turning into a chaotic mess? Unlike many of the self-help messages out there, we do not need to do everything at once. This is where I personally struggle. I feel pressure from all the self-help video shorts on social media and books to change everything in my life at once, and it just overwhelms me.

If we tend to the garden a little bit every day, it mostly keeps things from turning into chaos. We always have those instances where the tomato plant falls over because it got too big and there is a bigger issue to deal with, but overall, a little weeding here and water there every day tends to keep things on track for the harvest. In our lives, if we tend to the home and our family members and the things we are responsible for little by little, it will keep things manageable. So typically, before we turn on the video games or Netflix and grab that beer and book to chill, we should think about what little things need tending to so they do not blow up into larger issues. What chores or projects, if done a little at a time, would eventually be completed? As my dad would say, "First we work, then we play." Take a few minutes to do some of that work. Depending on the day, it is often much easier to keep the momentum of work going instead of having to start all over again. I'd encourage you to finish up your work before you relax for the day.

To clarify, when I say work, I am not referring to our kids. Even though it can feel like work, we shouldn't let our minds view children as anything but a joy. One of the joys that children bring is the ability to play, no matter what is happening. I often find myself doing a small bit of work around the home when I am off my nine-to-five, and the next thing I know, I am knee-deep in a game of sorts with my kids before dinner, having a grand ole time. It is almost like my children know that work will be here tomorrow, so I should let it be and enjoy my life.

After dinner and the evening activities, we still need to end the day and let our heads hit the pillow. I could throw in some personal opinions here of "Make sure you are involved in the nighttime routine" or "You do not go to sleep until everything is taken care of," but this is all subjective to your realities. (I would encourage it as much as you are able to, though.) When lying down, think of the day and all that transpired. Think about what you enjoyed, and let it lead to gratitude to God in your heart. I know you will fall asleep faster and have a more restful sleep with gratitude being the last thought in your mind at night.

The Sabbath Is for Rest

After working all week long, we are exhausted. Luckily, God built in a day of rest. Frankly, I think the Sabbath is very underutilized. People still work and do things on this day, and it makes sense why burnout is so prevalent in our culture today. God created the world in six days, and on the seventh, he rested. If God rested, so can you. Really, what could be so important on the weekend that it can't wait till Monday? Some of us work where our weekends are not actually our days off. If that is you, find what day works for you and your family to prioritize a day of rest.

There is so much I can write on this topic of the Sabbath, but I want to focus on one piece. Enjoying what you have. The Sabbath, as I see from God's example on the seventh day of creation, was designed as a rest from work, for you to enjoy the fruit of your labor. You worked hard all week parenting, working for an income, and tending to the garden of your life. How about taking one day to enjoy it all? Spend time with the wife and kids playing and being present. Go out and do something or buy a fun little meal to enjoy the income God blessed you with. Maybe even take a joyride in the Mustang you spend time rebuilding.

The Sabbath is God's way of helping us to remember him and all that we have because of his work in our lives. This mindset helps keep us mentally healthy by keeping our focus off ourselves and on God. When we get focused on ourselves, we can get discouraged pretty quickly. When we keep our focus on God, we get encouraged rapidly. Look at what you spend your week working on and find ways to enjoy it. If we do not find ways to enjoy what we have, we start to lose the feeling of being content. If we stop being content, then we lose gratitude. If we lose gratitude, we start to take our eyes off God and what he has done for us. The focus then turns to ourselves and what we are accomplishing.

Our family loves to do nothing on Sundays. We sleep, eat, and enjoy the day. The only things we do are go to church and maybe over to a family member's house. We do not clean, do dishes, work on projects (unless they are enjoyable ones), or really do anything other than what three little fun-loving toddlers require. A really good resource for anyone interested in more on this topic is the book Garden City, by John Mark Comer. It provides great insight into the Sabbath. Now all this I wrote is only a template of what I imagine a day could be like. It is very subjective, but hopefully you can see the baseline. We all have different jobs and different responsibilities.

Think about your priorities and take care of yourself, Dad. Spend time with God, your wife, and your kids. Be faithful in the job that God provided to you to work and the responsibilities entrusted to you. Carve out time to enjoy what you have worked on so that your heart is filled with gratitude and your eyes stay fixed on Jesus. This is the source of strength to not just make it but also to thrive, day after day.

CHAPTER 6

The Very Real Tension
of Priorities

Think about something you absolutely love to do or have.
Are you enjoying it, or has it started to enjoy you? What
is something in your life you do because you love it? Have you
noticed that you stopped loving it and only do it because you
sort of made a habit of it? As one of my favorite pastors and
teachers of the Word, Scott Nickell, once said, "When a good
thing becomes an ultimate thing, ultimately that good thing
becomes a destructive thing."

On that happy note, welcome to chapter 6! In this chapter,
we are going to cover the tension of priorities. It is great to
know whom we should prioritize and what a routine of our
day could look like, but how does that play out when life is
tugging at us? For example, as I experienced, what do we do
when we are faced with a paycheck that isn't cutting it, when
we have a family to take care of, but we love our job? Or how
do we handle substances and the silent destruction they start
to breed?

Since story is one of the best teachers, I want to get practical for a moment and share some of my story to connect some of the dots in your mind. In these examples, I felt the very real tension of how to prioritize, what to prioritize, and whom to prioritize. There will not be a time in our lives when priorities do not cause tension, and I hope my story inspires, encourages, and is relatable to you.

From personal experience, every day is a fight to choose the right priority, and it is a struggle. I don't believe there is perfection to be found with priorities. We will always have the circumstances of the day tugging at us, and we will decide our responses. If you are anything like me, my wants often win out, my love for substance holds me down, and my struggle to keep the right things the main thing almost seems impossible on most days.

Back in 2021, I came face-to-face with the priority posed by money, wealth, and career concerns. The decision in front of me was so foggy and confusing, it really didn't make any sense.

I was in my fourth year or so working in the ministry field for a pretty good-sized church. In the IT department, I got to do a lot of different tasks and talk to so many great people that it made it a dream job—almost. As most people in ministry know, you don't choose this career for the money.

I first started working for the church around the corner from where I lived at the time in winter 2018. Later that year, I was engaged and got married. We had very few expenses, and my wife was able to work, so the church salary worked great. A quick note that I want to point out is I firmly believe that no matter what you do for work, if you are following God, he will provide what you need and throw a sprinkle of just a little more on top just to bless you. But don't just take my word for it: "And God will generously provide all you need. Then you will always have everything you need and plenty left over to share with others" (2 Cor. 9:8).

I am not dissing the salaries of those at churches, but like any nonprofit organization, the church usually pays on the more conservative side. As time went on, so did our family. Our son was born in early 2020, right as the pandemic stopped everything. A blessing in hindsight was that my nonremote job turned completely remote the day I was supposed to go back to the office. Later that year, my wife returned to work part-time, and we were beyond blessed to have free childcare for those two days she worked. (Thank you to those special few who assisted if you are reading this book; you helped us in ways you cannot imagine.)

In the fall of 2020 through the spring of 2021, we experienced our first home-purchase adventure. This story is so big in itself, I might need to write a book about it. But in July of 2021, we were first-time homeowners, and living became tight. In August, there were no shifts for my wife to pick up for work, so we couldn't even cover our monthly expenses without dipping into our savings. We knew at the end of the day, we could keep a roof over our heads, food on the table, and gas in the car, but any type of extra things in life would go out the window if my wife was not able to pick up any work. I am not talking about luxury items but everyday expenses such as car repairs, house troubles, or the cost of health and wellness.

It was around this time I started questioning my priorities. See, something didn't add up in my mind. How could I be following God and prioritizing him, much less working for him in the place I deemed most spiritual, and see life not heading in the direction of stewarding and providing and taking care of what he had entrusted to me? Those things were my wife, son, and home at the time. I was thinking, "Maybe working at a church isn't 'working for God,' as one would think it is."

Don't get me wrong; of course, working for a ministry or church is a great thing! However, as I have discovered, it is easy to get your priorities out of whack in the name of serving God.

As life continued, I noticed that my paycheck was not going to cut it anymore to support my growing family, and an extra raise was nowhere in sight due to normal budget limitations. There were also extra demands that would take me away from my family during big times to spend together as a family, like Christmas and Easter. These requirements and what God was leading our family to prioritize were starting to clash. I learned these two lessons during this time: (1) The number-one goal in life is about pursuing your personal relationship with Jesus, not getting paid to work for a place that tells people about him, and (2) stewarding what God has given you, including in your family, is more important than making sacrifices of the responsibilities entrusted to you in the name of Jesus.

I have a challenge for you. No matter where you work, ask your spouse and kids, if they are old enough, if your work seems like the priority over them. Ask them if your job is interfering with leading your family or providing for them as they need. I do not want any dad to be known for working over being with his family. One looks good in the eyes of your peers; the other makes a difference in the souls of your wife and children.

From the fall of 2021 to the spring of 2022, I was job searching. I knew I needed a job that provided more income to support and steward my family better. In order to follow the priorities that my wife, Kelly, and I decided as a family God had for us, it was time to pursue some changes. Job searching took a grueling nine months, and I interviewed so much that I became a pro. When I was starting to give up hope, God provided an amazing job that (1) was an ideal pay raise, and (2) was a 90 percent work-from-home job. Talk about an amazing turn of events!

Even though it was hard and I could not do it perfectly, I didn't give up on trying to keep my focus on the priorities God showed as important. My pursuit of these ended up leading to a place of being able to prioritize them even better, which I did not think was possible. I have to keep reminding myself— and maybe you do too—that when you are keeping what God says is important, God will take you to a place where you can continue to do that and flourish.

What changes in your life are you scared to make when it comes to money or career? Has the pursuit of money or career jumped too high as a priority in your life? If your life is overwhelming and anxious, or if you are not able to spend time with God, your spouse, and kids like you hoped, maybe it is time to reevaluate your priorities. Money and career are good things, and we must remember that God takes care of it all. Money is a tool to help take care of what he has entrusted to you, but we have the responsibility to steward it well.

Fast-forward a couple of years, and we arrive at another situation where my priorities are being challenged. This time, it is the priority of wife, kids, and self. It is the year 2022, and I love alcohol, mostly beer. I started brewing my own beer, bought wine-making kits, and frankly did not think twice about how many substances I was consuming. Through the cold winter and into the fresh spring of 2022, I unfortunately developed an unhealthy habit of drinking too much.

When I say drinking too much, let me clarify. I think most of us go to the far end of the spectrum, thinking about people who wake up and need a drink right away. Or we think about people who let their substance abuse or addiction lead to neglect of their families and jobs and the domino effect from there. Even though these are true stories and serious issues, I was not that person. I would say I was in a much more dangerous place. I drank too much often. Drinking is socially accepted, so it allowed me to get good at hiding how much I was consuming.

Every parent knows about the humorous jokes about mama juice, a.k.a. wine, or how at the end of every long day, a glass of cheap wine is a reward. "What about dads, though?" I ask myself. It seems society sends the message that dads can drink, no matter what they do, or they are not manly enough if they can't handle their liquor. If the game is on, drink. If you are hanging with the guys, drink. Not feeling manly enough? Drink more and drink harder.

Here is where we pick up the story.

In late spring of 2022, I developed a habit (as the great country song "Drinking Problem" goes, "I had no problem drinking at all"). Worse yet, I was superb at hiding it and abusing it where it was socially accepted. During the day and afternoon, I did not drink, but after the kids went to bed most nights, I grabbed the keys, hopped in the car, and drove around the corner to the local liquor store. Perusing the aisles, I searched for the beer that stood out as the one for the evening. At the checkout, I would have my six-pack of beer, some wine, or potentially even some shooters. I was ensuring that I would have enough to drink that evening. After I got home, I would drink and watch TV, completely enjoying myself. Making sure not to drink too much, I was not getting blackout drunk or even to the point of wondering if I drank too much, but I was drinking too much, daily, for weeks. This tape was on repeat, and sadly over the course of months, there were probably only a handful of days alcohol did not touch my lips. I was on the road to disaster.

When out at lunch or dinner on the weekends, it was not uncommon for wine or beer to join the lunchtime festivities, and I will never have a problem with that. I believe there is nothing inherently wrong with alcohol itself, as it is just a drink, but how it is used needs to be weighed with the utmost caution. For example, abusive drinking will lead to major health and relational problems, but enjoying it in moderation could be a pleasurable experience for those who like a drink.

Unfortunately, I went from moderation to abuse. This was my life. I was prioritizing substances, and it was deceiving me and those around me. In June of 2022, I think God was starting to open my eyes to the fact that there was a problem, and I started paying attention. I distinctly remember God telling me during a teaching at church, "If you want to be free, give it to me" (it was alcohol). I felt like a slave to alcohol. It controlled me. It was so dangerous because I was so good at hiding it and deceiving myself and others that everything was okay. This culture we live in has made drinking so socially acceptable that it is nearly impossible to tell when someone has a drinking problem.

So I decided to quit. That lasted about eleven days. Then I'd drink again for a while, then stop again for a while, and the cycle repeated itself. Month on, month off, week on, week off, and so on . . . my efforts were futile. This went on for a whole year and a half to the present day, which covers some of the timeline to which I have been working on this book. I want to be transparent here. I am in the midst of breaking down a priority that got out of shape in my life. Living the life I know God has called me to has been a struggle for eighteen months and counting. So if you are reading this book and talking to me in your head, saying that change can never happen, I've been there. Change isn't possible on your own and does not happen right away.

The only way I can explain how I am slowly changing is that someone else must be changing me. I'm not trying harder, and I'm not disciplining myself when I mess up. We all see people doing the "75 Hard challenge," diet plans, and other workout programs, only to find themselves back in old habits after their timeline is up. Unless there is a heart change, there is no permanent change, and I hate to break it to you, but you can't change your heart. Only Jesus can, and he does when you spend time with him day after day, intentionally seeking him.

Jeremiah 29:12–14 states, "'Then you will call on me and come and pray to me, and I will listen to you. You will seek me and find me when you seek me with all your heart. I will be found by you,' declares the LORD, 'and will bring you back from captivity'" (NIV).

This verse was written to the Jews in captivity then, but think about your situation. Does it feel like captivity? Instead of asking the question what is holding onto you, ask yourself what you are holding onto. I felt captive to alcohol and was longing for freedom. Little did I know that it was me keeping myself in captivity. It was through a continual and imperfect eighteen-plus months of continually seeking God for change in this area of my life that I finally arrived at a spot where change is happening. Change looked like finally being humble enough to attend a recovery group, letting in friends and family to where I was really at, seeking wise advice from trusted individuals, and attending counseling. No, it has not been perfect, but I know I am on the path that leads to the freedom I have been searching for.

I wrestled between the thought of whether I needed to pursue complete sobriety or if I was able to just enjoy alcohol in moderation. Through counseling and other introspective work, I landed on keeping alcohol moderated in my life instead of cutting it out completely. I learned a valuable lesson that God seems to have weaved into all his creation, and it is this: boundaries lead to freedom. Adam and Eve, in order to enjoy their garden freedom, had to maintain a boundary of not eating from the tree in the middle of the garden. I implemented boundaries, and that is where I felt freedom.

I will cover this more later in the book, but counseling was a large contributor to my healing. Of course, Jesus is the ultimate Physician, and he changed the parts of my life only he could, but counseling provided the tools necessary for changes I was in control of. I encourage anyone who can't seem to break through any addiction or troublesome issue in their life to go to a few sessions to have someone else guide you on your way. It was through a counselor's guidance that my issues with alcohol were brought to light, and I felt like I had a light-bulb moment. Confessing my issue to those around me and seeking a group of people I could trust for support was also a big help. So make sure to get other people involved in your journey; you can't go this alone.

Alcohol derailed me from giving quality to the priorities in my life. I was able to keep the priorities in order, but they were suffering because I was suffering. Experiencing dueling priorities, as I call it, is like not having a priority at all. If what you are called to do has to split time with something else, then your calling can never fully be what it is supposed to become. I do not wish this on anyone.

So what priorities are you feeling tension between?

I can probably think up and write many more stories where my priorities conflicted and I had to deal with the tension. Most guys, I think, deal with money and some sort of dependency. What is that for you? Fill in the blanks and evaluate how that is impacting the priorities in your life. Are there changes that need to be made? Who needs to be let into your journey?

We can do it, fellow dads. I know this because with God, I was able to figure some things out. Each obstacle I faced took time to resolve. Please don't give up if change isn't happening right away. Give God time to do his work, which we cannot see.

I hope this chapter was a glimpse into how priorities play out in life and into how the tension between them is real. If it weren't for the pursuit of God and his revelation to me of changes I needed to make in my life, I would probably never be writing this book, and who knows what all I would have lost? Hopefully, you can see that whatever becomes ultimate in your life can destroy you, and that is exactly what Satan wants to do.

Jesus, however, came to bring life and life to the full. Both Jesus and Satan want things for not only you but also everyone connected to you. Jesus wants your home and family to flourish, while Satan does not.

Wondering what type of man it will take to fight off Satan from his attacks? Wondering what it is to even be a man? Then chapter 7 is for you. Becoming who God designed us men to be is crucial in this fatherhood journey. Once we understand our role as men, we will better be able to fight and recognize

Satan's attacks against us and our families. The next section starts our section on tools for success. Now that we have the characters that matter and a map for our time, it is time to hand you some tools.

PART 3

TOOLS FOR SUCCESS

CHAPTER 7

Work Your Responsibilities

I n December of 2023, I was listening to a sermon and was thinking the whole time how I could post about all that I was learning from it. A voice almost as clear as day strongly and gently said, "Stop! Stop! This is for you, take it in. Be selfish for a minute." I reckoned it was the voice of God telling me something.

Constantly praying for God to teach me new things about him to apply in my life, I rarely gave it a second thought when I spent time with him and I learned something. It stopped there. See, we can learn things, but if we do not spend time applying them to our lives, they do not stick. Then we ask, "Where is the growth?" This cultural age we are in is obsessed with information and followers and online presence. I fell for it; I still fall for it.

Before I explain this, let me give a little recap.

We just finished the second leg of the adventure through this book, focusing on time, also known as priorities. I broke them down and provided practical examples from my life; I hope you have a better understanding of the way God has created relationships. When I first became a dad, it took me a couple of years to realize there was a priority order, and then I had to adjust my life on the fly. If you are reading this book before your little one arrives, or if you already have a nest full, just know that it takes a little help from everyone around you to keep you on the path of priorities. It takes intentionality and encouragement. It "takes a village," as they say.

This chapter builds upon chapter 2, so if needed, reread chapter 2 before you start or maybe review it after you end. Jesus can change us, so if any of this seems impossible or unrealistic, I assure you that through God's power in your life, all is possible.

To quote Francis Chan, "We need fewer voices and more examples." As mentioned in my story, I was really good at learning and becoming another voice. Recently, I was convinced that I was so focused on my voice and telling everyone else what I learned that I became a really good virtue signaler. Unintentionally, I was obsessed with knowing all the right things, and I didn't pay much attention to what I was applying in my life. I was getting too excited when I heard a new bumper-sticker quote from a sermon or catching phrase in a Christian podcast.

Why do I mention this? Before we get into the subject at hand to learn, I want to encourage you to be selfish and really take in everything I write. When God has something for us, let it be for us. Let's work on it, apply it, then share it. Don't share it and never apply it. Like Chan said earlier, "We need fewer voices and more examples." Let our lives speak volumes through applying what God is teaching us. It will speak louder than we could ever post or speak about. It is not that I am writing revolutionary words, but what can God speak to you and teach you in the rest of this chapter? Take a moment, pray, and ask God to do just that.

So what is a man? Who is a man? What is the most basic definition of manliness? Besides muscles and good looks, what key characteristics did God create men with that makes us different from women? Really think about this. When God was making Adam, he created him in such a way that he later needed to make a helpmate for him because Adam was incomplete. Therefore, Eve was created different from Adam. Obviously the body chemistry was different, but there must have been different character traits as well that were uniquely woven into men and women. What are they?

One place where I found to have learned what the differences were between men and women was at any Christian men's conference, retreat, or getaway. The topics covered usually hammer home the fact that men were created to provide and protect, and it usually ends there. I want to push back on this. I am not saying we do not have a calling to do those things, but I do not see that as being what sets us apart as men, but rather a role we expand into once another is placed in our care. Before Eve existed, there was no one to provide and protect. It was just "single and ready to mingle" Adam. When God created Eve, Adam's responsibilities shifted to include provision and protection of those entrusted to his care. But notice, his responsibilities expanded from his initial task at hand, as Genesis 2:15 explains: "The Lord God took the man and put him in the Garden of Eden to work it and take care of it" (NIV).

What can we conclude from this verse? Responsibility is what you were designed to carry as a man, and the tool God gave us to do this is work. We work our responsibilities.

I am challenged, encouraged, and inspired after reading this verse. Manhood is wrapped up in the simplest, yet most challenging, task: working your responsibilities. What separates boys from men is when we get serious about working the responsibilities given to us. Think of your life, even back to your high school days. We all had responsibilities, but we didn't always work all of them. I mean we tried, but our focus was mostly on ourselves and what we needed and what we wanted. (Okay, maybe it was just me.)

I'm not sure about all the family situations out there, but looking back, I see that my dad was teaching me to work my responsibilities. He gave me chores that challenged my work ethic, and he pushed me to do hard things. In the moment, I thought life sucked, but looking back, I see the training that was taking place.

Culture's voice is loud, and even the Christian subculture voice is. I remember noticing this in my late teen years. Maybe I am on an island by myself here, but all through late teen years, I was not preparing for working responsibilities. I was preparing to have them. People kept telling me I was going to have a wife, have children, have a home, and have a career. I was preparing to have all of those and was totally naïve to the fact that in order for them to thrive, they would need work, or they would all die.

John Ritenbaugh from The Right Use of Power explains Genesis 2:15 with a unique perspective: "God has given man powers to carry out the responsibility that has been given into his hands: to have dominion. Man must do the following: Put what has been placed into his hands through a finishing process, watch over it, guard it, protect it, and preserve its beauty."[3]

Wow, this is amazing. Think about how this impacts the ways we are a husband, a father, a friend, a son. This pushes back on culture's take of fatherhood like none other. If we rework this quote a bit, we might end up with something like this:

- Man must help his wife through a finishing process, watch over her, guard her, protect her, and preserve her beauty.

- Man must help his children through a finishing process, watch over them, guard them, protect them, and preserve their beauty.

- Man must bring his home through a finishing process, watch over it, guard it, protect it, and preserve its beauty.

- Man must bring his responsibilities through a finishing process, watch over them, guard them, protect them, and preserve their beauty.

What does this mean? To start with, I believe this is the work to be done to your responsibilities.

---

[3] John W. Ritenbaugh, "Commentaries: Forerunner Commentary, Genesis 2:15," Bible Tools, bibletools.org, accessed December 9, 2024, https://www.bibletools.org/index.cfm/fuseaction/Bible.show/sVerseID/46/eVerseID/465.

Finishing Process

"Bring them through a finishing process." Now this, to me, sounds weird and complicated. The only times I can imagine what this means is when I am thinking of staining a table or painting a room or building a LEGO set with my kids. These items are incomplete, in need of some tender loving care and order. For the table, room, and LEGO set to be brought to completion, I have to work by adding to them with what I am given. I must apply the stain, roll the paint, and assemble the pieces. In this example, I was given tools, equipment, and instructions to ensure I could complete these masterpieces.

Transition to the masterpieces around you. God has given you tools, equipment, and instructions on how to help bring his masterpieces to completion. What are you doing with what he has provided to you? Do you know he has given you what you need already to do the work he has called you to? Look at your hands. To quote my wise dad, "Stretch out your hands in front of you. Take a good look at them. Tell yourself, 'These hands are gifted.' So try and you will be surprised at what can be done by taking one step at a time. Do not be afraid to try the unknown."

Unlike a project, we will not be able to bring people to completion. That is God's job. Our job is to do our part by joining in with the Creator bringing his creation forward, helping it become a part of his incredible world.

Philippians 1:3–6 states, "I thank my God every time I remember you. In all my prayers for all of you, I always pray with joy because of your partnership in the gospel from the first day until now, being confident of this, that he who began a good work in you will carry it on to completion until the day of Christ Jesus" (NIV, emphasis mine).

He is the final one to complete his masterpieces, but that does not mean we have a free pass to neglect our part. All through this book, I am writing the theme that God is partnering and doing this with and through us. This is no different. God is sharing the responsibility of bringing his masterpieces to completion and invites us to join in. He is doing his part, we need to make sure we are doing ours.

So what tools, equipment, and instructions has God given you for your masterpieces he entrusted to your responsibility? Well, besides the spiritual tools and disciplines that we will cover later, I believe this is a case-by-case basis. We are all created unique and different, but we have what the people and things around us need. What is your talent, your spiritual gift, your resources around you? Perhaps where you feel most weak is your greatest strength because God says where you are weak, he is strong. Look at your kids and your wife; you have something they need. God created you on purpose, with purpose, and for a purpose. Create an environment that will help bring those masterpieces God gave you to completion. Every good environment that is thriving has good protection around it to keep the bad out. Here, we expand our role from not only builders to protectors as well.

Watch Over, Guard, and Protect

These seem pretty instinctive to most men. I mean, we love a good movie where the main character has these responsibilities related to someone coming against them. Usually, there is a good beating that happens to the wicked foes, and we all feel so pumped up afterward, as we are resonating with what we see. Imagining protecting, guarding, and watching over our loved ones against physical opposition is something that just makes us feel manly sometimes.

Some of us, though, think about this and probably feel anything but manly, but God still calls us to our families' physical protection. You do not need to be six feet five, weigh in at 240 pounds, and be completely shredded. Sure, that helps, but it isn't everything. God built into you the ability to defend your home physically. Lean into it, believe it, and be prepared. Pray that nothing ever happens, but you must be willing to get into it if something does come against your family.

But what about the spiritual protection for your family? Yes, there is protection, guarding, and watching over needed there too and it is the real battle we face. As Paul writes to the Ephesians in chapter 6, verse 12: "For we are not fighting against flesh-and-blood enemies, but against evil rulers and authorities of the unseen world, against mighty powers in this dark world, and against evil spirits in the heavenly places."

Some practical ways to be aware of spiritual warfare is to ask yourself a few questions. Who or what are you letting into your home? Are there people in your life or the lives of your children whom you are letting into your home who are influencing against God? Is what is being consumed via the many media outlets we have access to (like streaming services, music, or books) sharing messages that go against what God says is to be right and true? We often blink and miss these, as what is so wrong with a little language there, some inappropriate media there, and so on? That is what Satan wants us to think. He whispers little lies in our ears, "It isn't really that bad" or "Are you really going to be that kind of Christian?" and "Who is going to know?"

Compromise in what you let into your body and your home through what you see and hear will eventually land us in a place where we wonder how we even got there. Sound familiar? Whenever you hear about a pastor or someone whose life just blew up and you could never see it coming, it means that at some point in their journey, they did not fight back against the simple yet convincing lies of Satan. Simply put, they did not engage in spiritual warfare. What started out as what seemed like an innocent seed grew and eventually took that person out. Kill the lie; fight back against the darkness when it is in infant form before it overtakes you or your family.

Another example: Are you praying over your family and home? Demons are real and are all around, doing the work of Satan. Prayer is a powerful tool that we can use to intercede and ask God for help. I am not a theological guru on this topic, but I have studied it enough to know that we can ask God to send protection to cover our lives and our homes and fight off the power of darkness. To quote Paul again in his letter to the Ephesians, "Pray in the Spirit at all times and on every occasion. Stay alert and be persistent in your prayers for all believers everywhere" (6:18).

Watching over, guarding, and protecting means doing this in both the physical and spiritual. If we do one and neglect the other, then the masterpiece in our care is at risk for the enemy to kill and destroy. Seem like too much? Read John 10:10.

As it states in 1 Peter 5:8, "Stay alert! Watch out for your great enemy, the devil. He prowls around like a roaring lion, looking for someone to devour." Satan is after us and our masterpieces. He wants to physically and spiritually come after anything God created. This is why we must be aware of fighting on two fronts. If you are only protecting one front, then do not be surprised if the enemy ambushes you from the back.

Fighting on both fronts is hard. But as with any fight or battle, there is training to be done beforehand. How are you training to physically and spiritually protect your home? Being physically fit is a very good thing to be training for. Perhaps even training to yield a physical weapon of some sort that you plan on using is wise. Disciplining yourself in spiritual matters can help prepare you on the spiritual front of the battle line. These spiritual disciplines can be turned into weapons. Do you know how to use them? In chapter 9, I write about ways to battle spiritually.

Preserve Their Beauty

Now what the heck does "preserve" mean? The best analogy I can think of is a really good jam or jelly, which was preserved perfectly for my morning toast and cup of coffee. This jam had so much good flavor and texture that it only got better after sitting for a while, perfectly preserved. Hmm, interesting thought, isn't it, when we apply it to our responsibilities?

The Cambridge Dictionary defines preserve: "To keep something as it is, especially in order to prevent it from decaying or to protect it from being damaged or destroyed."[4]

Now that is good! Preserving is the summary of bringing your responsibilities through a finishing process, watching over, guarding, and protecting them. As we are helping move

---

[4] "preserve," Cambridge Dictionary online, dictionary.cambridge.org, accessed December 9, 2024, https://dictionary.cambridge.org/us/dictionary/english/preserve.

our masterpieces into the forms that God has ultimately designed for them, we must learn to preserve them on the way.

There is beauty to be found in all of God's creation. The responsibilities in our realm were created by God and thus are beautiful. We get to apply this preservation to these beautiful wonders God has blessed us with. Work is good and will be the way in which we get to preserve the beauty of what we have been given.

The words preserve and persevere seem very similar to me. How often are we going to get tired of doing the work? If you are like me, a lot. But we do not quit! We must persevere in order to preserve. I started praying a lot for perseverance over perfection recently because I am noticing I could not care less that I can't do things right, but I need strength to keep going and keep working. Romans chapter 5 talks about how perseverance produces character and that character produces hope. That hope is Jesus.

So what is it to be a man?

As easy of a definition I can think of is this: A man is one who perseveres to work his responsibilities.

I have seen many good men give up on perseverance. Life takes a toll. They started off so well in their marriage and fatherhood, but as the adversity stacked up and blow after blow struck like a heavyweight fight, they just did not get back in the fight. This is why it is so important to have Jesus at the center of your life as your strength. This is why it is so important to be training physically and spiritually for the battle we are in. You never know what fight will show up on your doorstep, but you have to be ready. However, you can only rely on yourself so much, and you cannot be a man without God. Adam did not only rely on himself, and he would not exist without God. Why do we think it is any different for us?

God is who makes you a man. Culture does not get to define you as a man, your dad does not get to define you as a man, your friends do not get to define you as a man. Your wife, your mom, your kids, your neighbor, your boss, your coworker, your social media, your humor, your strength, your job, your car, your truck, your hunting expertise, your love for sports, your ability to drink—you name it!—none of these things get to define you as a man. Only one voice may, and that is the voice of your Creator. He created you as a man. Now rise up to the challenge and let him do his work.

CHAPTER 8

We Are Not Alone

T he 2015 Rose Bowl stadium was nearly completely filled with fans rooting for the Oregon Ducks football team. The Florida State Seminoles had a couple of sections devoted to their garnet color, but they clearly were not the fan favorite. Second half, Jameis Winston, the FSU quarterback, scrambled around, then fell backward and fumbled! The Ducks recovered and took it to the house for the score! Oregon was up big now on FSU and making a solid case for punching their ticket to the national championship. You should have heard the crowd. The Rose Bowl was not a large stadium, but could it ever echo the noise of thousands cheering. I was in the middle of a section of mostly students, and it was all high fives and spilled beer. It was one of the best game environments I had ever been a part of.

The crowd was completely fixated on what was happening on the field, and people were cheering their hearts out for the men executing the plays, running the distance, and making the tackles. These college kids were playing in the best game of their life so far, and they had thousands of people at their back telling them they could do it and to keep going. They were bringing that extra oomph to help them overcome their tough circumstances.

Now wouldn't that be great if we were doing the dishes when we didn't feel like it and a crowd erupted behind us cheering us on that we could do it! Imagine walking into that boss's office to quit a toxic job, but instead of fear and anxiety about the future, this crowd showed up with an eruption of encouragement and a "We are behind you" feeling that the boss even felt it and was scared to even stand in your way. What if we are watching our child be born and are filled with, "I don't know what I am doing" feelings, then this crowd shows up again, shouting, "You got this!" and "MVD, MVD! [Most Valuable Dad]"? I think if we had this happen, we would do a lot more of what we felt like we could never accomplish. Also, I think we would not let the enemy win in our mind and keep us anxious or depressed for way longer than need be.

However, these emotions for dads are a very present reality. How many of us dads feel alone, depressed, anxious, overwhelmed, overstimulated, or burned out, like we're dragging our feet, speechless, doubting our abilities, or just flat-out tired? I know it has to be a lot of us, because every dad I talk to mentions feeling like this multiple times, week in and week out. Turn over to social media, and you will find forums, groups, and influencers supporting dads feeling this way. It is a reality that being a dad is hard work and it wears on you. Support is what we need, but it seems impossible to find. Even when it feels so lonely, the Bible leaves us hope that we are actually not alone: "Therefore, since we are surrounded by such a huge crowd of witnesses to the life of faith" (Heb. 12:1).

Did you know this thought of a huge crowd cheering us on is not a fantasy of what could be better, but our reality?

This is what I picture it is like when you place your faith in Jesus. Picture any NFL, NBA, NHL, or MLB stadium or even an MLS or other soccer stadium, and you appear on the goal line on one end of the field. You look around and see a sold-out stadium chanting your name and cheering you on. You feel dazed for a moment and then start stumbling toward the other end of the field. It's just you and the crowd. Every time you fall, the crowd is still there. Every time you run in circles, the crowd is still there. Until you get to the other side, the crowd will still be there, cheering as if you had only begun.

This is a beautiful picture and is why I wanted to write this chapter on this topic. Thus far in this book, I have covered a lot. It might feel a bit daunting to start trying to make changes in your life, or maybe it seems like an impossible task to even start. Don't worry; you've got this.

In my journey of moderating drinking, as I mentioned in an earlier chapter, I had a moment like this, and it has carried me. I was in the kitchen doing dishes after a long day, and all I could think about was going to the store to buy some beer. Of course, my heart did not really want it, but everything inside me screamed, "Just a little bit!" I bent over to put a dish in the dishwasher and then stayed bent over with my hands on my knees like an exhausted athlete who needed to catch their breath. I prayed. "God, please, please give me strength to make the choice I want to make."

It was as if Jesus heard my prayer and was like, "Oh shoot, I know just what he needs!" He quickly scrambled over to what I like to imagine as the "Thoughts of Jesus" library or something, grabbed a thought off the shelf, and flung it like a Frisbee right to my brain . . . and it landed just in time. Plunk!

I envisioned myself standing in a stadium bent over and tired with my hands on my knees, thinking I can't go anymore. Then I stood up and took one step. Roaring like I never heard before, a crowd appeared out of nowhere. I felt an energy surge through my body. I began thinking, "I can do this!" The one step I took was not drinking that day, and the crowd of witnesses knew what was up, and they wanted me to hear it.

Standing back up, I resumed my dishes and I threw on some songs from my worship playlist.

This huge crowd of witnesses has been right where we are. They stared at their struggle in the mirror and had to finish the race themselves. They know the struggle is real, and they want us to know we can make it. So why would the author of Hebrews not share details in the verse we read? Well, I never shared the full verse; here is more (Heb. 12:1–3):

> Therefore, since we are surrounded by such a huge crowd of witnesses to the life of faith, let us strip off every weight that slows us down, especially the sin that so easily trips us up. And let us run with endurance the race God has set before us. We do this by keeping our eyes on Jesus, the champion who initiates and perfects our faith. [a] Because of the joy [b] awaiting him, he endured the cross, disregarding its shame. Now he is seated in the place of honor beside God's throne. Think of all the hostility he endured from sinful people; [c] then you won't become weary and give up.

We are not sure who the author of Hebrews is, but the author and this crowd are encouraging us to get rid of the weights slowing us down, making us run in circles, and tripping us up. These, of course, are metaphorical and are speaking to things in our life we know are not from God and are holding us back from experiencing all that we can. In order to have the endurance and perseverance to finish the race, sinful and unwise choices need to be dropped.

For me, drinking became a sin issue over a substance issue and it needed to go and be put back to its appropriate place in my life. I am somewhere on this journey. I can feel it as a weight slowing me down, holding me back, and making it so tough to endure and persevere. When I stopped abusing drinking, I experienced freedom in ways I cannot describe but would feel very similar to dropping dead weight when you are running. You get a second wind, you get a pop in your step, and you feel like you can run faster than you ever thought possible.

So for me it is drinking, anxiety, and need for control, and this list probably goes on, but this is what I am immediately working on. So what is it for you? Is it a substance problem? Is it lying? Deceit, jealousy, your career, your own wants and desires that do not align with what God says is right and true?

Luckily, we are not left wondering how we can do this. We are reminded to strip away every weight that slows us down. Some of these weights are obvious, and others are not. If we know God says lying, for example, is not a good practice, then it is easier to see that it is a weight slowing us down. But what about the more complicated or unseen weights? How do you know if you have one of those? Well, let me share from experience.

For the longest time, I have always lived like life is good and there is nothing wrong. There is no sense poking around at what ain't broke. At least that is what I thought. Slowly, over time and years, I noticed friends and family started pointing out areas of my life I should be paying closer attention to. To stick with a football analogy, friends and family were my linemen, blocking for me and making a path where I could run the ball of fatherhood. It was incomplete, though. Every time I got tackled and bruised, there was no doctor or trainer. No professional to give me a wellness check when I received a blindsided tackle that left me dazed on the ground. But I did have teammates, a.k.a. trusted friends and family. They always picked me up and helped me discuss strategy, encouraged me, and got me back out on the field

I finally got to a point in my life where I recognized the need to expand my team. In order to get ahead of some of the unknown weights in my life, I knew I should probably get a counselor. However, out of pride mostly, I took over three years to finally sign up and go to my first session.

I know I might have lost half of you by mentioning that dreaded C word: counseling. Perhaps therapy is your triggering word of choice. I think there are three main responses to this topic: (1) being in denial and saying counseling is stupid, (2) thinking it is trendy and everyone is doing it, so therefore hating it or being overly obsessed with it, and (3) actually knowing what it is and how it can help you. Have you ever worn something and later that evening, someone says that your shirt is inside out or your tag is inverted? I know I have. This is similar to working with a counselor. There is so much that happens in life, and we may be picking up weights and tying them to our waist, but unless someone—in this case, a trained professional—can point it out and ask why we are carrying it, we just assume that is how we are supposed to function.

Counseling seems very self-focused, and that personally irritates me because I think we should not be focused on ourselves. But being focused on yourself for a bit of time to take inventory of your past, which informs your future, is important. To know where we picked up weights that slow us down, we have to look back on our lives and the circumstances we navigated. As for being a Christian, this is where I say counseling is pretty awesome. Let me explain.

While working in a counseling session, my counselor helped point out a weight I was carrying that I did not know existed. To be brief, but provide a practical example, this was around my adoption. In the first eighteen months of your life, how you receive care is critical to how you will view and interact with relationships in your life. My counselor was able to point out along with my own reflection that my normal tendency is to think that people need something from me, but I do not need anything from anyone. Interesting, isn't it? I then turned these thoughts to my relationship with God.

Do I think I do not need God? How is it that I believe and follow God if my tendency is to think I do not need relationships in my life? These questions started to plague my mind, but I could only come back to the thought of God's grace. I believe that God allowed me to view him how I needed to; after all, he knew I needed him. For those moments growing up when I felt isolated and lonely, I always knew in the back of my mind it was not true. He was with me. It was in these moments when I turned my attention to God, as he would never leave me and he wants me. In all the moments when I felt like the relationships around me were letting me down, I was able to count on God to not let me down. When I look back on my life, I see an endless number of times when he was there and kept his promise he would never leave.

This is why I think counseling as a Christian is a blessing. You have a chance to reflect on God's grace in your life. Honestly, you will uncover brokenness in counseling, but if you are a follower of Jesus, you will hopefully start seeing God's endless grace upon your life, even when you didn't deserve it. Having someone who can point out weights in your life that you picked up without knowing is an incredible help, so if you can afford to even do it once a month, I promise the return on your investment will be tenfold.

(Quick pause for a challenge: I can hear arguments already forming in your minds against the cost of a counselor. Let me just put it this way. What we value, we find a way for. Excuses can be left at the door. I know this all too well, as I was in the boat of "I can never afford to go." But I was wrong. Turns out, you just restructure your budget to prioritize your values and you make it work.)

Okay, back to the chapter

So now I have linemen and a trainer. Linemen are the trusted friends and family we have in our life to block and carve out a path for us to run. But I also have my trainer, my counselor, who can bandage me up and point out ways that I was running wrong to make me more efficient and dangerous on the field.

Join me as we work our imagination for a moment. Picture yourself scared to go to counseling, nervous in the session, or trying to find the right words to confidently describe your situation. Fill your mind with the crowd cheering you on that we mentioned before. Did it give you a small spark of strength? Now fast-forward a few years, and you have been in counseling a little while now. You have uncovered a few things in your life, and now you feel yourself ten pounds lighter, as those discoveries were able to drop ten weights you did not know you were carrying. How does that make you feel? Observe your surroundings twenty years from now. You are in a situation you thought you would never be able to handle, but this time it is different. You hear the army of voices in your mind encouraging you, and you are walking into the fight more in shape than you have ever been. Do you feel more confident than ever before?

Translate these thoughts into fatherhood. If you are like me, it is a task in which, most of the time, I have no idea of what I am doing. Anxiety and depression easily take over most days, as I think I have screwed up my kids or I am doing everything wrong. But this new way of thinking has given me hope. I no longer feel like I am doing this alone, and I am finding weights I picked up that I am negatively parenting from. I want this for all of us, hearing the cheers and encouragement from brothers in the faith who have gone before us and dropping weights that are hindering us. I imagine and hope for a new wave of dads free from the chains holding us down and charging freely into fatherhood. I am not sure the last time I talked to a dad who was confident in his parenting. I want to see this change. I am hopeful and confident we will start seeing a wave of dads acknowledging the hardship but still believing in themselves. Most importantly, I look forward to all dads knowing we are not alone anymore and we have support, even when we feel the most alone. It will be through Jesus that there will be a breaking of generational curses and allowing our ceiling to be our kids' floor.

What can we practically take away from this chapter? There are two things to pay attention to. First, know that with Jesus, you are not alone. Not only is he with you, but there is also a whole crowd cheering you on. Next time you are having a hard time feeling lonely, remember this and close your eyes for a moment. Picture those faces of encouragement. Second, it is time to invest in trusted relationships. You need to build your team and, if possible, hire a professional. Back in the chapter about priorities, I mentioned the importance of other

Jesus-follower relationships. These will be the friendships you want to pursue. Even though non-Jesus-followers can be great friends and offer great wisdom, they will lack what it means to follow Jesus and what he teaches. This could lead you in the wrong direction if those are the only close voices you listen to. I have been working on this for a long time, and relationships are hard. I get it. However, I have not given up, and I pray you do not quit either.

It is time for change! It is time to get our confidence back. That time is now! The crowd is roaring; you are on center stage. Fatherhood has been placed in your hands, and it is your turn to run and make the play. Friends, family, and counselors are out there to block for you, direct you, and bandage you up from injuries. Just like in a football game, you will have a breakaway and seem to score easily. On other days, you will have a ten-yard loss on the play. In each scenario, the crowd does not stop cheering for you or encouraging you to keep on, and your teammates around you do not quit on you. The support system you have been searching for is here!

Did you know that one day, you will cross that finish line of the race of fatherhood? You may be battered and bruised, but you will get in the end zone or run past the tape. You will climb into the stands, and when you turn around, you will see many dads running the same course you did, and you will have nothing to do except cheer and encourage them too. For you know what it has been like and what they are encountering. You know they can do it, and you just can't cheer loudly enough.

CHAPTER 9

Spiritual Armory:
Tools and Weapons for Battle

How many of us as kids enjoyed building different creations? I personally was obsessed with LEGOs. On any Christmas or birthday, if I got a LEGO set, I instantly ripped the box open, grabbed the instructions, and methodically started preparing my workspace and organizing the parts to make the building process easier. My fingers were my tools to fasten pieces together, and my teeth were of good use for when I squished the wrong pieces together and needed to separate them. (Looking back, I'm glad I did not chip a tooth; LEGOs are no joke!) As we know from any project, it requires tools.

As we dive into this chapter on tools, something to keep in mind is that these only work on the foundation set already in this book. Think of it like kitchen appliances: You can't use a spatula to fasten two pieces of wood together with a screw. The same applies here. These tools and weapons are spiritual disciplines that only work with following Jesus.

When one googles "Christian spiritual disciplines" or the like, results pull up a variety of disciplines. Here is an example as CRU, a popular Christian ministry formerly known as Campus Crusade for Christ, has nicely put together: Bible, prayer, worship, generosity, fellowship, fasting, silence, simplicity, and celebration. I am not honestly sure if these are all of them; I just know the small few that I practice routinely.

Learning and applying what I learn is important to me, so I will be honest that I have yet to put into practice all these disciplines, and I only practice a few somewhat well. A good perspective to have in this chapter is this: learn everything, but take your time and be intentional to apply one thing at a time. I will refer to these disciplines as tools from here on out. The words tools and weapons are interchangeable. These spiritual disciplines can be used as a tool to build a fortress for safety against the enemy or as a weapon against him. A weapon is also a tool, depending on how it is used.

Why are these important, and what do they have to do with fatherhood?

John 15:4–5 states, "Remain in Me, as I also remain in you. No branch can bear fruit by itself; it must remain in the vine. Neither can you bear fruit unless you remain in Me. I am the vine; you are the branches. If you remain in Me and I in you, you will bear much fruit; apart from Me you can do nothing" (NIV).

God does not leave us hanging out to dry; he provides tools to grow if we so desire. I can't be the only guy out there who likes tools. Whether they are tools for mechanics, yard work, technology, sports, guns, or creativity, all men have an obsession with tools to get the job done. Along with getting the job done, we have always heard it said that men just need to fix things. We grab our tools and set out to fix whatever needs it. God wired men to build, fix, and solve the problem.

Tools are our "go-to." Is it a coincidence he provided spiritual tools? As the professor in The Incredibles says while Dash is in the principal's office . . . "I think not!"

As I can see and have experienced myself, men seem to have a hard time knowing what it is to grow in their faith or how to do it. I see wives asking their husbands to become the spiritual leaders of the house for her and the kids, and the guy is eager, too, but won't admit he does not know how. That is why this chapter is key and is my paramount chapter. I want every dad and husband to know how to grow in their relationship with God, thus becoming the spiritual leader of their home for their family.

Being a spiritual leader just means going first; it does not mean being perfect or having perfect discipline. It means going first, admitting failure, asking for help, and not stopping. When the wife asks us to lead our family or the like, I want us to have the confidence to say, "Yes, and I know how!" We could view this chapter as "Tools to Success: How to Win at Fatherhood."

Reading the Bible

First up is the Bible. I am twenty-nine at the time of writing this book and have been a Christian my whole life. But to this day, I have yet to read the Bible from cover to cover. Recently, I have started this journey, and it has been amazing, but more on that in a moment. Let us first answer the question "Why is the Bible important?" It is God's Word. If it is his Word, then that means he is speaking. The author of Hebrews puts it this way: "For the word of God is alive and active. Sharper than any double-edged sword, it penetrates even to dividing soul and spirit, joints and marrow; it judges the thoughts and attitudes of the heart" (Heb. 4:12, NIV).

The words in the Bible are not just words; they are God's words. Something happens when you read the Bible as opposed to any other piece of literature. It is almost too complicated to explain, but there is a simple concept that sums up the complexity of the matter. Ask yourself this question: "If I read the Bible every day for a year, for fifteen minutes a day, how would my life be different?" Pause right now and ask yourself this question. If you have never read the Bible before, dream about what this might mean for you.

When I think of this question, I immediately think I will be a better dad and husband. I will have a better understanding of who God is and the story of life. My understanding of how God's world works will be deeper, and I will have insights into God I would never have had otherwise. These are just to name a few. Even this small list is inspiring to me to spend time reading God's Word every day.

When my daughter June was born, we watched a sermon online in the hospital room, and the church was in a Bible series at the time. The speaker, Doug Wekeman, asked this question, and it inspired me. From that day on, I have done my best to read God's Word every day. Honestly my Bible reading streak maybe never passed eight days in a row, but, boy, did I start reading more. Guess what happened? I started learning things about God, and my life, and how to interact with life all around me so much better! The small list of thoughts I had about what could be started to become my reality. In my new reality, I noticed there was more room for growth than ever before. This also means I discovered that one will never arrive! "Whoa there," you might be saying. Never arrive? What does that mean? It simply means life is so complex and God is so infinite that we could spend the rest of our lives reading the Bible, and it would still be as if we only just began to understand him and his world.

As I began to read through the Bible from cover to cover, I started understanding who God was at the beginning of time and noticed he is the same today. I noticed his plan for humanity, his desire to be with his people, and so many other things. This is why I do advocate for reading the Bible from cover to cover in a timely fashion. You can read a Bible reading plan found online, or you can do what I do and read two chapters a day from two different books of the Bible. You could read two chapters chronologically a day, and two chapters of another book, just for variety.

It is like a snowball. As a snowball rolls down a hill, it gathers more snow and more momentum, and goes faster and farther. It is the same with reading the Bible: once you start disciplining yourself to read it, you start gathering momentum and you just can't stop. You encounter God for who he is, and once you experience God, you can't stop. You experience love, joy, peace, patience, kindness, and so many more things. It's kind of weird to say, but you get addicted to it in a sense.

So if the Bible is a tool, what does it help fix or fight against? It helps with perspective. When we understand who God is and what he says, we view our situations and lives differently. Whenever you sense you need a new perspective on a situation, spend time in the Word, and God will open your eyes to what you need to see.

After all this hearing from God through his Word, you might want to say something back in response. This leads us to our second discipline: prayer.

Prayer

I find this one is the easiest for me to engage in. Talking without ceasing, I picture myself as my toddler with endless words flowing from my mouth. Praise God for his patience is all I can say. But this is what prayer is: just talking to God. There are two ways I discovered we can pray, and I want to share those with you. Even though we can pray any way we want, I think there is something special to the way Jesus spoke about it in Matthew.

The most common version of prayer is the Lord's Prayer, as we find in Matthew 6:9–13: "This, then, is how you should pray: 'Our Father in heaven, hallowed be your name, your kingdom come, your will be done, on earth as it is in heaven. Give us today our daily bread. And forgive us our debts, as we also have forgiven our debtors. And lead us not into temptation, but deliver us from the evil one'" (NIV).

This template for prayer from Jesus is profound because it helps guide our conversation. It is very important to acknowledge the order that Jesus speaks about how to pray. Starting off, Jesus says to recognize who God is. We get our focus off ourselves, our problems, or anything that might be clouding our mind when we approach him in prayer. Next, we proceed to ask his kingdom come, his will be done on earth as it is in heaven. This reminds us of our mission here on earth. We want to be able to help bring and grow what God's kingdom in heaven looks like here on earth. After this, our focus is on God as our sustainer—not just for our bellies, but in every area. We acknowledge that all we have is because of him. Now this part I find most interesting. After we focus on who God is, remind ourselves of our mission, and recognize God as our Provider and Sustainer, we then ask for forgiveness.

This intrigues me because I personally feel obligated to start every prayer with repentance and forgiveness, even if I have no idea what I might have done wrong. I feel like God doesn't want to hear from me unless I am "in right standing." But we can see here that God doesn't ask us to confess our sins before recognizing him as our Father. It is more important that we know who he is and who we are to him over what we must do. This shows me we are loved, no matter what, and we have to believe it. Now that is a good Father.

The prayer ends with "Lead us not into temptation and deliver us from evil." I have heard an explanation that this is a way to ask God to lead us. The Bible says that he will never tempt us, so it is not asking for God to not tempt us. When I read this, I think about asking God's guidance away from evil and situations that I might blindly find myself in where temptation is all around me.

If you are hoping to pray with this and can't remember all these details, memorize the Scripture. If it is in your mind, you will be able to recall it at any time. Also, if you read closely, the prayer is divided into two sections: remembrance and asking. We start off remembering who God is and praising him, our mission to make disciples, and our role in creation, and remembering who sustains our every breath. Asking for provision, forgiveness, and guidance wraps up the prayer.

Let me share how this template practically helped me. If you are like me, when I come to God in prayer, I usually need something. Recently, I just had some major repairs on my car that depleted our cash reserves. The technician noted there was one more leak that would cost $3,300 to repair. To say I was beyond myself is an understatement. My immediate reaction was to pray because I didn't know how we were going to pay for this. I remember it going something like this:

"Lord, praise be to you! You are the Maker of all things, and all things are held together through you. The sun rises and sets on your command, and for you to recognize me in all of your splendor, I am grateful. You are greater than all else in the earth or anything I can comprehend. God, your kingdom come here on this earth as it is in heaven. Help me to be a part of bringing your kingdom here. Let me be on a mission to expand your kingdom and have eyes and ears to see and hear where I can make an impact. Jesus, I remember that you sustain us and are our Provider. I ask for our daily bread today. All that we need, please provide. You provide our health, our abilities; our every being is sustained by you. I know you will give us what we need in every area, not just physically. Can you please forgive me for the ways I have sinned, even the sins I do not know I committed? Please forgive me for those and show me where I am blind. Lord, lead me not into temptation. Guide me in the way to go, away from evil and on the path that leads to life with you."

My brain after a prayer like this was no longer concerned with what I thought was an overwhelming situation. Instead, I was filled with peace and assurance that everything would be okay, for I remembered who my God is. He provides all the time, and my mission here on earth is greater than any car repair.

The second way I pray fits into this part of the story. I believe we can talk to God like a child to a dad. Be honest and open, letting him know how you feel and what is happening. After all, he is our Father. During this situation, I was playing Ping-Pong between using the Lord's Prayer and using child-talking-to-Dad prayers.

My child prayers were something like, "God (Dad), I don't know what to do, but I know what you promise. Not sure how all this is going to work out. Can you please help? I either need money or a miracle. You know what is up, and I don't. Please, please, please come through. You know we have stuff coming up that we are saving for, and I'm not sure why you wouldn't want us to have those things. This can sink us. I just don't know what to do right now . . . amen."

Well, fast-forward a few days, and the Lord did a miracle. I got a second opinion from a trusted mechanic, and he noted that I did not indeed need to spend lots of money fixing the car. Instead, I could rest easy and maybe fix something in five years. I threw up a child-to-Dad hallelujah prayer and was on cloud nine!

On the back end of what I thought was a terrible situation, I realized it was through prayer that I was able to trade feelings of anxiety, restlessness, and confusion for peace, stillness, and direction. This is why I love the Lord's Prayer and child-to-Dad prayers. They are powerful tools.

Worship

Well, I love me some worship. There are times in my life where I just need to have the music on in the background or intentionally to bring some peace and ground myself back into reality. As I think about worship, I believe worship through song specifically gets us back into the presence of God. I won't get into the weeds of worship, but I'll just share how worship helps me.

Recently, we went camping with the kids and it was an adventure. The first night we were there, we forgot the pack-and-play for our eighteen-month-old daughter. She is a lady of routine and comfort, so sleeping on a large bed wasn't really going to be her thing. We were nervous, but we put her to bed at the end of the day, and she seemed to sleep fine. A little into the night, she woke up. There were night terrors and screaming. Barely able to be comforted, she needed someone with her to hold her as she slept. I decided to go for it and sat with her. Trying to sleep, I wedged my back against the side of the pop-up trailer and closed my eyes when I could. Every few minutes, it seemed, she woke up and needed a pat on her back and some love to fall back asleep. This went on all night long, and I probably slept about an hour. My son somehow slept through the screams all night long, and I was so very jealous. It had been such a long night. I decided through the night to not even look at the clock so I did not get discouraged by how little I was sleeping.

Eventually, June was able to sleep on her own in the early morning, but then at 5:30 a.m. when the sun popped up over the lake, she was ready to go for the day. I, however, was not ready and frustrated and wanted to quit the camping adventure with our extended family and just go home. I knew I needed something to ground me back in reality, letting me know that everything was going to be okay.

I turned on my Bluetooth speaker and clicked Play on my worship playlist. "Time and Time Again," by Mack Brock, started playing, and almost instantly, my soul felt peace and comfort. I saw my kids differently, saw the sleepless night differently, and witnessed the sunrise on the lake differently, and everything was instantly transformed into a beauty that was incredible and just about impossible to describe. In that moment, I believe through worship music I was transported into the presence of God. Maybe I wasn't actually transported. We are always with God, but when we put on worship music, it helps transport our physical being to where our soul rests, and that is in the presence of God. So now when my physical self saw an early morning that I was not ready for, my soul felt the beauty of being in God's presence in a special and new way.

When we find ourselves in moments we just need Jesus, we have to turn to worship. Our souls are always in the presence of God, and to get our physical selves in that position, too, worship is the tool to get there. Ask anyone—when chaos is all around and that worship music starts playing, our eyes quickly move from being focused on ourselves to being focused on God. This is powerful. Many times when I have anxiety from not knowing how to parent, I need to remind myself that God is parenting through me and is with me.

Fasting

Another great tool for experiencing the presence of God is fasting. I think worship is good for moments, but fasting is for a period of time. I used to practice this discipline routinely, and it did wonders for my soul. I did one of those thirty-day fasts where I just ate at dinner, and it was an amazing experience. Up to that point in my life, I had never fasted and never knew what it was. At the end of the thirty days, I journaled about my experience: "Fasting showed me that I spent a vacation with Jesus instead of just getting together for coffee, beer, or a meal." Let me explain this a bit more.

When you fast, you are, over a period of time, denying your physical self what it wants to access to get what your spiritual self, a.k.a. your soul, needs. This leads you to be in an almost constant state of living from your spirit. Remember I mentioned earlier that our souls are always living in the presence of God? Fasting leads us to a state of remembering that we are not just a physical body and living in a broken world. Instead, we are souls experiencing the presence of God fighting a battle against flesh. Our souls are in a physical body, fighting to live under the authority of the Holy Spirit. Picture a tug-of-war, with a physical body / the flesh on one side, the soul as the marker in the middle, and the Holy Spirit on the other side. We are being pulled in both directions, and spiritual disciplines help move us toward the spirit and living from out of it instead of in the flesh. Paul wrote the following to the church in Galatia about the tug-of-war between spirit and flesh: "But I say, walk by the Spirit, and you will not gratify the desires of the flesh. For the desires of the flesh are against the Spirit, and the desires of the Spirit are against the flesh, for these are opposed to each other, to keep you from doing the things you want to do. But if you are led by the Spirit, you are not under the law" (Gal. 5:16–18, ESV).

Generosity, Fellowship, Silence, Simplicity, and Celebration

When we fight back against our physical nature, these all battle the flesh and its earthly desires. One does not have to do complicated math to figure out what areas of life these help with. Selfishness, keeping to ourselves, and loud living are just a few examples. It comes natural to us to be self-focused, and that is the opposite of kingdom living. Kingdom living is about living from the spirit, which in turn shows us the answer to many of life's greatest questions. Do you desire the answers to life's questions?

As I am doing as well, you can continue to learn these other spiritual disciplines. Perhaps you will master them and write to me about your journey. You may even learn it so much you decide to write a whole book on it to share with the world. I'd encourage you to do that.

Don't worry; when you start applying these disciplines to your life, you will start seeing answers. Seems like a lot, though, doesn't it? That is okay; it is to me as well. Especially if you are newer to following Jesus, this can seem daunting. But don't worry! I know you can pick these tools up and start using them. Keep in mind that it will feel weird or odd when you first pick them up, as with any tool, but the more you use it and practice with it, the more comfortable you will become and know which tool to apply in different circumstances.

These are the few spiritual disciplines I have used over my life so far. As I mentioned, I am in the process of learning about the others and implementing them. This whole book is about sharing what I have done or am actively doing to be authentic and share a real-life story of a dad who is trying to figure it out. I will not pretend to be someone I am not or provide advice on something I am not actively practicing or at least understanding.

So, Dad, the next time you are having a moment (as I am sure you will soon), remember the tools and weapons in your belt. Read the Bible to shape your perspective, pray intentionally to take on God's truth about you, and worship and fast to satisfy yourself in his presence. It will rejuvenate your soul.

If you take all of this and intentionally apply it to your life, you will begin to experience change and grow in incredible ways. You will look back on your life and the circumstances you went through and be amazed at who you have become. It is impossible to use a tool every day while building and have nothing to show for it after a period of time. However, it is a choice to use it, and that is a decision only you can make.

Knowing that this book is about to end and wondering what final words I should leave with you, I spent a long time pondering how I should end the book. Many of the topics covered in this book leave us with a decision, so I will end the book casting a vision for us. What does it lead to, or what will it look like when we choose to apply what we have learned in our journey? Turn the page to discover the inspiration you have been waiting for.

Conclusion

A Tale of Two Trees

Once upon a time, there were two seeds. Both were perfect seeds, healthy and in good shape, and in great condition to become the amazing trees they were destined to be. One day, they were planted about fifty feet apart. These two seeds were planted on the edge of a beautiful lake.

As the years went by, these two trees popped through the soil and started growing. There were moments of intense storms and peaceful, growth-focused springs. The storms that came tested the trees, with wind, snow, hail, lightning—you name it. All the storms visited these trees upon their growing up. But they did not stop them; they kept growing. After the storms they endured, there were moments of peace and fruitful weather, which fueled their growth.

Twenty-five years later or so, these two trees matured. The tree on the left was beautiful! There was foliage like no one could believe. Many branches stretched far, and many leaves were fully green. Critters of all shapes and sizes called this tree home. The squirrels ran up to their nests and down to collect food. Robins found sanctuary in the branches of the

113

tree to raise their families. Bugs and raccoons also included this tree in their lives. Even humans benefited from this tree! They parked their trailers or tents under the tree, thanking it for the shade as they overlooked the grand lake.

This tree, however, was not perfect. Even though it provided much life, rest, and peace to others around it, there were scars. The storms left notches where there used to be tree branches. They even left some branches leafless. You could tell this tree had grown strong and tall, but not without a few stories of its own.

The tree on the right was very similar to the tree on the left. It had endured the same storms and trials. It was also just as tall and majestic as its fellow tree. But there was a major difference. There were no critters or humans enjoying its shade, nor even a single leaf calling the tree home. This tree was barren, with no leaves or flowering branches. Why was this?

Even though these trees were planted close together and endured the same type of growing up, there were factors that led to these differences. Perhaps it was the soil or how much it was watered. We do not know for sure, but we do know that what comes in through the roots will eventually be displayed high above for all to see.

For Bible scholars out there, does this story sound familiar? If anyone is familiar with the Parable of the Sower, here it is.

Jesus told many stories in the form of parables, such as this one (Matt. 13:3–9):

> "Listen! A farmer went out to plant some seeds. As he scattered them across his field, some seeds fell on a footpath, and the birds came and ate them. Other seeds fell on shallow soil with underlying rock. The seeds

sprouted quickly because the soil was shallow. But the plants soon wilted under the hot sun, and since they didn't have deep roots, they died. Other seeds fell among thorns that grew up and choked out the tender plants. Still other seeds fell on fertile soil, and they produced a crop that was thirty, sixty, and even a hundred times as much as had been planted! Anyone with ears to hear should listen and understand."

The story concludes (Matt. 13:18–23):

"Now listen to the explanation of the parable about the farmer planting seeds: The seed that fell on the footpath represents those who hear the message about the Kingdom and don't understand it. Then the evil one comes and snatches away the seed that was planted in their hearts. The seed on the rocky soil represents those who hear the message and immediately receive it with joy. But since they don't have deep roots, they don't last long. They fall away as soon as they have problems or are persecuted for believing God's word. The seed that fell among the thorns represents those who hear God's word, but all too quickly the message is crowded out by the worries of this life and the lure of wealth, so no fruit is produced. The seed that fell on good soil represents those who truly hear and understand God's word and produce a harvest of thirty, sixty, or even a hundred times as much as had been planted!"

These two illustrations demonstrate what? Have you noticed what is in common? If you guessed the roots, you would be correct. You may say soil, but that is what fed the roots. In the case of the parable, the good soil led to a plentiful

115

harvest. In the tale of the two trees, it is what fed the roots that led to the difference in plentiful maturity.

My question to you is this: What is feeding your roots in your fatherhood journey? Culture and what it promises, or God and what he promises? What will twenty years down the road reveal? Are your roots plugged into good soil full of nutrients, or plugged into soil you think is good but really isn't? We can trick ourselves into thinking our roots are planted where they need to be, but do not kid yourself: time will reveal what you were feeding on.

As I began this fatherhood journey, I started to realize things in my life needed to change. I was rooted in some good soil but was also aware that I was lying to myself and tricking myself into believing I was set up for success and good to go. Things needed to change. I needed to uproot and replant some of my roots. Having discovered some foundational changes that needed to be implemented, I took note. Thinking of my future, I realized there were parts of my life and the way I was beginning fatherhood that would have led to a somewhat fruitful tree. But I wanted to be a plentiful tree, full of as much abundance as possible.

Even though the abundance is way beyond our control, there are things we could do to set ourselves up better. Think about saving for retirement. If you do nothing, you will have nothing. If you save 10 percent a year, you will have a better chance at a better retirement. If you saved 25 percent a year, you would even have a better chance at a good retirement compared to the other two choices. Life happens, and there are no guarantees, but what we put in will reveal itself over time. God is the ultimate factor of any plentiful harvest, but God does ask us to put our skin in the game.

John 10:10 states, "My purpose is to give them a rich and satisfying life."

We know this verse sometimes is heard, "I have come that they may have life, and have it to the full or I came that they might have life and have it abundantly." Whatever the translation, the message is the same: God promises an abundant life like tree number one. Even though it is up to God how things turn out, he promises abundance, and we must hold onto that thought and that promise in the darkest days of our lives. We will get through it, we will overcome, we will experience an abundant life if we are rooted in God. Abundance doesn't mean riches or fame, but that life where we know we are full. It is hard to explain it, but we will just know.

I deal a whole lot with a need for control. This is most evident during our bedtime routine with the kids. Whenever I get on the fritz of not being able to control a situation, I get intense and angry. I have been working so hard for so long at addressing this. I consider this my 10 to 25 percent of saving for retirement. I am not sitting on my hands and not doing anything, but I am trying my best to address some changes. If this leads to abundance, that is up to God. I know, however, that this will lead to a better life than not addressing this area in my life at all. So far, I am noticing changes in my life, and it is easier than it was before to control my anger and lead with grace. Changing me from the inside out—the only explanation I have for this is God's grace.

What will the tale of two trees tell in your life? Evaluate everything you have read in this book and cross-reference it with your life. Imagine about twenty years from now. What do you see in your vision? Will it be a tree full of abundance and fruit or barren and dying? The choice is yours. The choice is ours. If there are changes, are we willing to do the hard work to uproot some areas in our life and replant them into plentiful soil? We have the opportunity to rethink God, ourselves, our spouses, our children, our time, and everything else in God's world. There is room to repent, replant, and weed out the garden.

This is a valuable time and space in this book to stop and take inventory of your life. Grab a pen and start journaling after you finish this book, or just do it now.

- What differences do you want to see in your life?
- How do you want to be known as a father?
  - What legacy do you wish to leave?
  - What are you willing to sacrifice to have this legacy?
- Are you willing to forsake culture's message of fatherhood and pick up a better, more abundant, life-giving message?
- What can you start doing today to start growing in your relationship with God?
- What can you start doing today in regard to your relationships and priorities?
  - God
  - Yourself
  - Wife
  - Children
  - Fill in the blank _____
- What can you start doing today to know you are not alone?

A life rooted in God is where to start. He is joining us on this journey, and he is the Author and Perfector of life and fatherhood. He wants to provide the nutrients you need. He will shelter you in the storms of life and provide rain and sun to help you grow. He knows how a tree grows best; team up with him. The strongest, tallest, and most plentiful trees are planted in the best soil. An abundant life is possible only with him.

It is time to rewrite the definition of dad, to tear down the message that culture has conjured up and embrace that it is time to take hold of an abundant, more life-giving message from the Creator of life himself.

The time for talk is over. It's time to power up and revive fatherhood forever, leaving a lasting legacy for generations to come.

Go change the world!

Continue the Journey!

T hank you for embarking on this journey through the pages of this book! The conversation doesn't end here; there's so much more to explore. To dive deeper into the topics we've covered, I invite you to join us on The Revived Podcast.

Visit RevivedBrand.com/podcast to access exclusive episodes, insightful discussions, and bonus content that will further enrich your understanding of fatherhood, truth, and personal growth.

Don't miss this opportunity to continue your journey. Scan the QR code and become part of a community dedicated to reclaiming and redefining what truly matters in fatherhood and beyond. Together, we can foster meaningful connections and support each other in this transformative experience.

Review Ask

Who else in your life needs this book? We must not keep what we learn to ourselves and must inspire others! Think of two dads in your life and share this book with them. Let's make that crowd in heaven even larger.

I have a vision that one day, we will enter heaven and will encounter the multitude of dads and others cheering us on. During this time, I will make my way to a high point to see below me and watch as dad after dad arrives behind us. There will then be a moment where hordes of dads start showing up. Wave after wave like a tsunami! I will think, "What in the world is happening? Is there an annihilation of dads happening on earth?" I imagine Jesus will hear my thoughts and find me in the crowd. He will put his arm around my shoulder, and in the purest voice I have ever heard, he'll speak. "These are the dads we have helped. So many fathers came back to me, and I helped change the world through them. Fathers turned their hearts back toward their greatest Father, began supporting one another, and taught their children to do the same."

Can we make this vision a reality?

If this book has resonated with you, please consider leaving a review on Amazon or wherever you purchased it. Your review not only guides me in improving future editions but also helps other dads discover this vital resource for navigating the challenges of fatherhood.

Share Your Experience

- What was the most impactful lesson you took away?
- How has the book influenced your approach to fatherhood and your identity as a dad?
- In what ways do you see it helping you leave a legacy for your children?
- Would you recommend this book to other fathers seeking guidance?

Or simply rate it with 1–5 stars!

Thank you for taking the time to share your experience and for being part of this journey to redefine what it means to be a dad. Together, we can empower more fathers to embrace their God-given roles and impact future generations positively.

Acknowledgements

I want to thank those who made this work possible!

First, as I mentioned in this book, without God, this book does not exist.

Dear Kelly, my beautiful and encouraging wife, without your support and strength, this book would not have been possible, and I would have given up on this task I believe God had for me. May all the men who read this book know that this work wasn't possible without you.

My children, without any of you, the joy to encourage others would have been lost. Thank you for reminding me of my mission every day as I wrote this book.

Brother Dave, David, you are a steady light for me. Many times, when I thought of giving up, I remembered you and the example you set of never quitting when it got tough in your own life. Because of this, I knew I could do it. An older brother you will always be to me, and I will always look up to you.

To my parents, your lives dedicated to following the Lord and listening to him will have an impact on eternity. When God told you to go adopt a little boy in a Lithuanian orphanage, you said yes, and the rest is history. Being brought into a home that loved Jesus was the best thing that ever happened to me.

Mom, your choice to homeschool us and work relentlessly with our skills was exactly what I needed in order to write this book. All of those hours I drove you crazy (during which you probably regretted schooling me) were for this moment.

Dad, I am at a loss for words to describe how much you mean to me. It is through your example of loving the Lord that I know who he is today. Not only have you taught me about Jesus, but you walked the walk, and that spoke louder to me than anything you ever said. I was watching you when I was little and when I grew up. I saw the same man, passionate about the Lord in any scenario. You inspire me in my marriage and in my parenting. Thank you for giving me the best guide for being a dad a man could ask for. You pointed and led me to the Savior, Jesus.

Matthew Mckenzie, your friendship is closer than a brother's. The many conversations we have had when you spoke truth and life into me during this process allowed for healing and grit. May you continue to speak truth to all you meet, and you will continue to change the world with God.

Jorgen Mandl and Zach Troyer, you may not know this, but I have sensed energy from you both. It gave me determination and excitement to get me through the toughest days in this work. Thank you both, and God be with you.

Spencer Marron, your willingness to serve me without really knowing who I was or what I was doing speaks volumes of your character. Your family is blessed to be led by you and your friends to have you as a companion.

D., your willingness to pick up a book and meticulously go over it could never be repaid. Your sacrifice to do this for me speaks to your character as a man after God's heart. Thank you for saving me from miscommunicating messages in this book and helping me clarify the points that were being made. Thank you for your example, your love, your encouragement, and your prayers.

To all the incredible family and friends whom I have talked to on this journey, I appreciate you. Thank you for your encouragement and support.

Author Bio

Steven Kolberg's passion for helping others discover their identity in Jesus and embrace the purpose God has for them has been a driving force throughout his life. Adopted from Lithuania at eighteen months old and raised in Colorado, Steven found that his personal journey shaped his deep dedication to fatherhood and family. As a father of several children, he often reflects on the joys and challenges of fatherhood, saying, "Sometimes I feel like I'm learning as much from my kids as they are from me."

Steven writes to share his insights with other dads, offering them practical wisdom and tools to embrace their roles as fathers, while building legacies that reflect God's plan for their lives. He is committed to helping men become who God designed them to be for their wives and children, grounded in faith and purpose.

When he's not writing or leading Revived, a platform aimed at reclaiming and redefining lives in Jesus, Steven enjoys life in beautiful Colorado with his wife and children. Through his work and personal journey, he continues to inspire fathers to step confidently into their roles, following God's calling with intention and purpose.

Now It's Your Turn

Discover the EXACT 3-step blueprint you need to
become a best-selling author in as little as three months.

Self-Publishing School helped me, and now
I want them to help you with this FREE
resource to begin outlining your book!

Even if you're busy, bad at writing, or don't know where to
start, you CAN write a bestseller and build your best life.

With tools and experience across a variety of niches
and professions, Self-Publishing School is the only
resource you need to take your book to the finish line!

Don't wait.

Say "YES" to becoming a bestseller:

https://self-publishingschool.com/friend/

Follow the steps on the page to get a FREE resource
to get started on your book and unlock a discount
to get started with Self-Publishing School.